Next-Level Accountants

Your guide to growing a firm of **trusted advisors**

MARY ELLEN BIERY

SAGEWORKS

5565 Centerview Drive
Raleigh, NC 27606
Phone | 919.851.7474
Toll Free | 866.603.7029
www.sageworks.com

Sageworks is a financial information company that provides risk management, financial analysis and business valuation solutions to accounting firms and financial institutions. Visit www.sageworks.com to learn more.

Copyright ©2016 by Sageworks Inc.

All rights reserved, including the right to reproduce this book or portions thereof in any form whatsoever. Requests for permission or further information should be addressed to research@sageworks.com. Free copies for individual use can be downloaded at http://web.sageworks.com/accounting/valuation/next-level-accountants/ebook/. Any brand names used herein are the property of the trademark holders.

This work is intended to familiarize readers with strategy and management issues related to accounting and valuation firms. It is informational and not intended to provide formal guidance or legal, accounting, tax or other professional advice. Every effort has been made to ensure that the content provided is accurate and helpful for our readers at publishing time. However, this is not an exhaustive treatment of the subjects.

....

Author | **Mary Ellen Biery**, *Sageworks*

Designer | **Elena Bondar**, *Sageworks*

Contents

1 | Charles H. Green
Want a Firm Full of Trusted Advisors? Do This, Not That

4 | Randall Bolten
3 Ways Trusted Advisors Communicate Numbers Effectively

8 | Kelly Phillips Erb
Share Your Expertise: Why It Pays and How to Do It

11 | Ronald J. Baker
Take These 5 Steps Toward Better Pricing

15 | Tom Hood
Create Time and Capacity for Advisory Services

18 | Marc Rosenberg
Motivating Partners to Develop a Firm of Trusted Advisors

21 | August J. Aquila
A Compensation Plan That Breeds Trusted Advisors

24 | Terrence E. Putney
Retaining Clients During a Firm Transition

27 | Allan D. Koltin
What Services Are Driving Our Industry Growth?

30 | Gale Crosley
Outside of M&A, How Will Your Firm Grow?

33 | Tim McDaniel
How to Develop a Growing Valuation Practice

36 | Jody Padar
Becoming a Future-Ready Firm

40 | Doug Sleeter
Ramp Up Your Tech Know-How

43 | Gary R. Trugman
Practical Advice for Scaling a Valuation Practice

47 | Joe Woodard
From Good to Great: Overcome Three Obstacles to Accounting Firm Growth

50 | Erik Asgeirsson
Mapping Your Tech Strategy

Foreword

Brian Hamilton
Chairman and Co-Founder, Sageworks

When I was in college, our first accounting book was *Accounting: The Basis for Business Decisions*, written by Walter B. Meigs. Reflecting now on college and my financial training generally, it is the subtitle of that book that captures my attention. "The Basis for Business Decisions" implies that accounting is not an end but a means to an end. Someone actually has to do something after the numbers are put together. Someone will make a decision about their business.

There are two primary reasons we finance professionals perform accounting and prepare financial statements:

1 | We have to. Businesses are required to submit accurate financial information as part of calculating and preparing taxes.

2 | To help us and our clients or managers make better business decisions.

I believe that most accountants and finance people perform well in the first area. The problem comes in the second, regarding business decisions, where I believe that many of us fail significantly. We are effective at preparing statements, then assume that our clients, bosses, employees and stockholders can actually make sense of them. This is often not the case.

As you probably know, business owners tend to be very good at generating sales and serving customers. They also usually know their products and services cold. But they are rarely good at understanding finance and accounting. And since many businesses don't have an external board of directors, they often lack objective feedback to help them avoid financial missteps.

Sageworks was actually founded in 1998 on this idea, and our goal has always been to help businesses make better decisions through a more comprehensive understanding of their financial health.

Businesses need your accounting firm to go beyond the traditional services of compiling financials or providing tax returns. They need your firm's input to make better business decisions based on their financial information, and they need your help identifying and building the value of the business. Studies have shown that business owners want a proactive, trusted advisor.[1]

All of this is probably no surprise to you, since you're reading this book. You also probably know that growing a firm of trusted advisors isn't easy. Like the business clients you serve, there are challenges that can prevent you from reaching your goals and taking your practice to the next level. You have time constraints, staffing needs, management issues and evolving technology—all competing for your attention.

However, as many businesses—including ours—have learned, it can be necessary and good to evolve your strategies, products, services and even resources in order to achieve bigger, better or sustainable goals. If your firm is in the process of that evolution, we want to help.

In the meantime, remember Walter Meigs! Your first job is to gather data and then present it accurately. However, your second and most important job is to present it clearly and succinctly and help your client/management team make better decisions.

---

[1] "What SMBs Want from Their CPA," Sleeter Group. 2014. Web. April, 7, 2016. www.sleeter.com/blog/2014/04/smbs-want-accountant-2014-update/

#NextLevelFirm

Introduction

Many accountants continue to run their practices the way they have been for years: focused on compliance-related services, battling compressed work schedules and lamenting pricing pressure. But a growing number in the profession agree that positioning firms as trusted advisors and delivering the services to support that strategy can produce more loyal, happy clients and staff, as well as higher revenues.

Timing for a change couldn't be better.

A 2013 research study[1] estimates that nearly half of total U.S. employment is at high risk of becoming automated over the next 10 to 20 years, and accountants and auditors ranked in the top one-sixth of the most automatable occupations. Meanwhile, high-paying jobs that are difficult to automate increasingly require social skills,[2] and many accountants admittedly have more confidence in their technical acumen than in their "soft" skills.

Next-Level Accountants: Your guide to growing a firm of trusted advisors brings together many of the accounting and valuation professions' top thought leaders to provide practical strategies to help firms continue to add value beyond their technical skills. We've tapped top experts in firm strategy, compensation, marketing, client relations, client retention and technology to hear their real-world advice for cultivating a firm of trusted advisors and for scaling an accounting business. The sources in this guide read like a "Who's Who" in accounting and valuation, with several of them named to *INSIDE Public Accounting's* 10 Most Recommended Consultants and many of them listed among *Accounting Today's* Top 100 Most Influential People in Accounting and various professional halls of fame.

Thought leaders such as Gale Crosley, Doug Sleeter, Tim McDaniel and Erik Asgeirsson share insight on the importance of serving as "quarterback" for your business clients: helping them identify needs and direct resources with the bigger picture in mind.

Jody Padar and Allan D. Koltin discuss approaches for providing a better client experience while securing your firm's future growth. Tom Hood, Marc Rosenberg, Joe Woodard and Gary R. Trugman provide practical advice about using technology, leveraging staff and focusing on "A" clients to free up time so you can work on strategy, management and other high-value work.

---

[1] Frey, C. B. and Osborne, M. "The future of employment, How Susceptible Are Jobs to Computerisation." Oxford Martin Programme on the Impacts of Future Technology. 2013. Web. April 7, 2016. www.oxfordmartin.ox.ac.uk/publications/view/1314

[2] Deming, David J. "The Growing Importance of Social Skills in the Labor Market." NBER. Working Paper, Aug. 2015. Web. Apr. 7, 2016. www.nber.org/papers/w21473

#NextLevelFirm

Ronald J Baker, August J. Aquila and Terrence E. Putney offer partner and practice-management strategies for transforming your firm's focus from commoditized, compliance work to value-added advisory work.

Finally, Charles H. Green, Randall Bolten and Kelly Phillips Erb share best practices for developing some of the "soft skills," such as communicating trustworthiness, that set apart trusted advisors from accountants holed up in an office and glued to compliance work.

Continuous learning and developing niche services are other themes here. And many experts emphasize that strategy must precede action. Whether your firm is adjusting compensation plans or evaluating technology, our experts say, identify the bigger picture goals first and make sure that your technology, plans and people support those goals.

Of course, we hope that as you evaluate technology, you'll consider Sageworks and its solutions—the ProfitCents suite of web-based financial analysis solutions and the commercial-grade, web-based platform of Sageworks Valuation Solution. Just as you are looking for ways to bring value to your clients, so are we. But even if you don't choose our solutions, we hope you'll find useful advice here that helps you pursue your own professional passion.

After all, we've worked with thousands of accountants and business owners over the years, and we know that accountants truly want to help their clients.

Mary Ellen Biery
Research Specialist, Sageworks

Mary Ellen Biery *is a research specialist at Sageworks, a financial information company, where she produces content for the company's blogs and websites, as well as for other outlets, such as Forbes.com and The Huffington Post.*

She is a veteran financial reporter whose work has appeared in: The Wall Street Journal, Dow Jones Newswires, CNBC.com, MarketWatch.com, Nasdaq.com and other sites.

Want a Firm Full of Trusted Advisors? Do This, Not That

Developing trust is complicated, but trust is the ultimate competitive advantage for winning and retaining clients.

Accountants may assume that the technical expertise and knowledge of your partners and staff are what set the firm apart from competitors, but Charles H. Green, who literally wrote the book on being a trusted advisor, says that is not the case. "Expertise is the entry requirement, the jacks for openers, the table stakes," he says. "But it's not the expertise that determines whether you get the deal."

Instead, what determines whether you win or keep the client is the trust you develop. Unfortunately, however, accountants sometimes unintentionally take approaches with clients that impede trust, says Green, founder and CEO of Trusted Advisor Associates, co-author of *The Trusted Advisor* and *The Trusted Advisor Fieldbook*, and author of *Trust-Based Selling*. This can mean not only lost business, but also undue scrutiny of bills and a relationship that becomes more adversarial than consultative.

Green believes that some accountants' efforts to convey expertise and knowledge to assure clients of the firm's competence can actually hurt the chances of building trust. Here are two situations to avoid, along with simple phrases Green suggests that accountants employ instead.

Charles H. Green
MBA

Charles H. Green is an author, speaker and world expert on trust-based relationships and sales in complex businesses. Founder and CEO of Trusted Advisor Associates, he is author of Trust-Based Selling, and co-author of The Trusted Advisor and the Trusted Advisor Fieldbook. He has an MBA and spent 20 years in management consulting (The MAC Group, Gemini Consulting.)

 @CharlesHGreen

DON'T: RUSH TO THE SOLUTION

"The biggest single obstacle I find over and over to creating trust is a perfectly well-intentioned inclination to rush to the answer too soon before having adequately listened to people," Green says. This inclination comes from a good place: The accountant wants to help.

"We have this temptation to solve the problem, to come up with the answer and to drive toward a solution, and the sooner we can give it, the better," Green says. "The unfortunate fact is that's not how people work."

Many people don't want advice or solutions until the advice-giver fully understands who they are and where they're coming from. This type of

> **" It's not the expertise that determines whether you get the deal. "**

#NextLevelFirm

understanding isn't about the advice-giver defining the problem by asking questions like "how big," or "how many" or "have you thought about," Green says. Instead, it's about listening "until the other person lets you know in no uncertain terms that you know them and you understand their problem."

Tell me more.

DO: ASK FOR MORE

Green says using three simple words can address this challenge: Tell me more.

"Sort of lean in, pay full attention and stop your brain from thinking what the problem is and just listen to what the person is telling you," he says. "Say things like, 'Tell me more about that,' or 'What's behind that?' or 'What do you think?' Of all of those, the best is just 'Tell me more.'"

Green notes that it's these kinds of questions that medical professionals ask during diagnoses, that negotiators use and that marriage therapists suggest. "Marriage therapists will tell you one of the biggest turnoffs in relationships is being dismissive of people or solving their problems without listening," Green says. "We all want to be heard before we accept advice."

"Obviously, it is still a problem-solving profession and we do have to come up with advice. But the biggest problem is doing that too soon," Green says. "It's helpful for an accountant to say, 'Before we jump to some answers, I want to make sure I understand your situation. Is there anything you haven't told me or am I missing anything?' Even just saying that makes the other person appreciate that you're trying to get the big picture. Then it's OK for them to say, 'Yeah, you have everything; you've got all of the information. What's the answer?'"

DON'T: OVERPLAY YOUR EXPERTISE

Another way efforts to reassure the client of your technical proficiency can backfire as it relates to trust-building is when an advisor places too much emphasis on their expertise. Is this possible? Green says it is.

He recalls a client who once described how his former Big Four firm lost out on a bid for an engagement, and when he asked the prospect for feedback on why, he got a surprising answer: A lack of trust. "So my client said, 'What? That's really hard to hear because we totally believe in trust and we're dedicated to serving you, and we really think we have the best and smartest team, and we've invested the most time to understand your situation, and you're telling me you don't trust me? I don't get it,'" Green recalls.

> "One of the most trust-creating things we can say is, 'I don't know.'"

"He told my client, 'We trust that you have really smart people—maybe the smartest people out there, and we trust that you'd bring together your best people for us. In fact, we trust that you're so good that whenever we get into a disagreement or an argument, we trust that your people are going to beat up our people every time—and therefore, we don't trust you.'"

That prospect was worried he would get steam-rolled rather than be assisted. Green says this illustrates how it's important for accountants to acknowledge occasionally that you may not have all of the answers.

For example, sometimes you may not think you're getting the big picture from the client or you may think the client is wrong about something and you don't know exactly what to say. "The wrong thing is to just bull ahead and tell them what you think without addressing the elephant in the room," Green says.

> Green suggests clarifying any questions or uncertainty by using these four simple words: **Please help me understand.**

DO: KEEP IT HUMAN

Green suggests clarifying any questions or uncertainty by using these four simple words: Please help me understand.

"Furrow your brow and say, 'Help me understand,' 'How come nobody's mentioned this?' or 'Maybe I'm missing something. It would seem you'd want to do so and so; please help me understand why that hasn't seemed to come up.'"

"One of the ironies is that we spend all of this time as accountants and consultants trying to show people how smart we are and how trustworthy we are. But one of the most trust-creating things we can say is, 'I don't know.'"

RESOURCES

- Free One-Minute Trust Tip Videos, Trusted Advisor website. http://trustedadvisor.com/trust-tips
- 100 Articles on Trust in Business, Trusted Advisor website. http://trustedadvisor.com/articles
- eBook: *How to Sell to the C-Suite* (download), Trusted Advisor website. http://goo.gl/PfTi1o
- Riding the Shark: Vanquishing Fear in Selling. Part 1 of 4, by Charles H. Green, Trusted Advisor website. http://goo.gl/9Ki6cD
- "Accountants win more clients doing these 3 things," Sageworks blog. http://goo.gl/CIJ9lb

#NextLevelFirm

3 Ways Trusted Advisors Communicate Numbers Effectively

Numbers are the cornerstone of knowledge for accountants and other financial professionals, but for many of your business clients, numerical information can be confusing or worse yet, meaningless. Consider how many clients admit they file away their financial statements or tax returns each year without ever looking at them again.

But unfortunately, clients who don't understand the numerical information are less likely to seek advice on handling opportunities or challenges revealed in the numbers. Furthermore, they may be skeptical of additional advisory services offered by their accountants, because they don't see evidence of a need for action. This equates to lost opportunity for the accounting firm, and it certainly doesn't cement your role as a trusted advisor to the client.

Randall Bolten, a former Silicon Valley CFO, CEO of Lucidity consulting and author of *Painting with Numbers: Presenting Financials and Other Numbers So People Will Understand You*, says that accountants and other financial professionals have a unique opportunity to build trust with clients by ensuring the numerical information provided is understood.

"There's a close relationship between your personal credibility and the credibility of the information you're providing, and this is true in every human relationship," he says.

People believe the information of people they trust. Similarly, if they come to believe some information, they come to trust personally the person who provided it.

"How much your audience trusts both you and your information," he says, "starts with having people understand what the information is."

"If your audience doesn't understand you, how can they trust you?"

Bolten says that how accountants and other financial professionals present numerical information is as important a part of client communication as is the way you use words when you write a note or speak to an audience.

"Every good communicator has a unique personal style that helps them be recognized and by extension, be trusted and respected and appreciated for their ability to communicate," he says. "We all remember people who are really good communicators. We remember the way they choose their words, the way they stand up and face their audience, the way they use humor and analogies."

Randall Bolten
MBA

Randall Bolten is the author of Painting with Numbers: Presenting Financials and Other Numbers So People Will Understand You and a long-time Silicon Valley finance executive. His 30-year career includes nearly 20 years as CFO for both public companies and startups, as well as senior financial management positions at Oracle and Tandem Computers.

Bolten is a frequent workshop leader and speaker, and writes extensively on communicating numerical information effectively. He is an instructor at U.C. Berkeley, and also operates Lucidity, his consulting practice. He holds a Bachelor of Arts degree from Princeton University and an MBA from Stanford University.

  @RandallBolten

" If your audience doesn't understand you, **how can they trust you?** "

#NextLevelFirm

> " How much your audience trusts both you and your information starts with having people understand what the information is. "

It's vital to develop a style of communicating numbers, so that when people look at your presentations of numbers, they know how to read them, according to Bolten. When your client knows how you typically present numbers, the things you consider important and where to look, they are several steps closer to understanding and trusting not just the data but the direction you provide.

Here are three tips from Bolten for communicating numbers effectively:

AVOID "GAAP-SPEAK"

Understandably, accountants have to present numbers in accordance with GAAP when it comes to engagements such as audits or financial statement preparation for investors. But Bolten notes that only a small share of financial information produced by companies has to be presented in accordance with GAAP. Most numerical information is used to manage the enterprise and not simply for compliance, and it won't achieve that purpose if management doesn't understand it. One way to help clients understand the numerical information is to avoid the jargon associated with GAAP.

"'GAAP-speak' is the equivalent of talking down to your audience or demonstrating to your audience that you know things that they don't know," he says.

Many small- and medium-sized accounting firms work with day-to-day financial information of companies that don't have large financial staffs to help them produce management information, so it's up to outside accounting firms to go beyond complying with GAAP and to help management understand the numbers.

Using words like "accretion" or discussing the finer points of expensing stock options doesn't help the business owner understand the company's future cash-generating ability. Remember your audience when you are presenting numerical information.

PROVIDE CONTEXT

Regardless of your audience, each member is pressed for time and needs contextual information to make sense of numbers when you give financial presentations. Producing an income statement with one column showing

#NextLevelFirm

just the current period's actuals is meaningless, Bolten says, "unless the people in your audience have photographic memories about the budget and about how they did last year."

Providing comparative numbers from previous accounting periods, forecasts or estimates can provide the context that clients need to make sense of the numbers. Contrasting the client's information with industry benchmarks or industry averages are additional options.

Bolten also recommends providing metrics so that your audience can immediately make better sense of the numbers. "Don't make your audience do work that you can do for them, like showing profit margins," he says. "Ratios are an immensely powerful tool for adding meaning and context to the raw numbers. Dividing one number by another is something we all learned to do in grade school, and we should do more of it in our numbers presentations."

REMEMBER THAT LOOKS MATTER

Bolten notes that many financial reports are nothing more than giant monolithic blobs of numbers, and that's inexcusable. It's like getting a three-page memo with no paragraph breaks. Taking care of the appearance of every memo, note or presentation of numbers to the client will make the information easier to understand and sends a message that you care about and respect the client, Bolten says.

This means paying special attention to how your information is laid out visually on the page, and choosing carefully the words that run across the top and down the side of a spreadsheet. "It's true that making information look good does take a little extra time. You may not need to be as obsessive as I am about how you present information, but you definitely need to pay more attention to the look and feel of your reports than most people do," Bolten says.

No matter how unimportant or *ad hoc* a report may seem, Bolten suggests, always imagine that you are preparing it for a board meeting. You will develop habits that will enable you to produce coherent, effective and great-looking reports even when you're under time pressure. "Roger Federer hits 2,000 practice serves every week. That's not because he doesn't know how to serve a tennis ball," Bolten observes. "He does it so that muscle memory will help him hit great serves even under the pressure of the fifth set of a U.S. Open final. Or, as Aristotle said, 'We are what we do repeatedly.'" And as an added bonus, that throwaway report sometimes actually does end up in a board package.

Making information more understandable takes effort and time, but the information provided in the process will result in great value to the client. "That information will get used, not only by the internal accounting staff that you interact with directly, but also by non-financial people inside the enterprise, like the sales people and the manufacturing organization. And it will be used by stakeholders like the banks lending or approving a line of credit or the board of directors trying to understand the business," Bolten

> "You don't get any credit for doing something that nobody else understands. You become a trusted advisor by giving people advice they understand."

#NextLevelFirm

says. When these internal players are able to tell the board or outsiders which firm helped them accomplish their goals, Bolten says, then this is how the firm actually becomes known as meaningful and trusted advisors.

"Accounting is a very technical discipline," he notes. "It's hard. But you don't get any credit for doing something that nobody else understands. You don't become a trusted advisor that way. You become a trusted advisor by giving people advice they understand."

RESOURCES

- Website: Painting with Numbers. http://www.painting-with-numbers.com/
- *Painting with Numbers: Presenting Financials and Other Numbers So People Will Understand You*, by Randall Bolten (John Wiley & Sons, 2012). http://goo.gl/L7jG8A
- Overview video of Randall Bolten discussing many of the issues related to communicating numbers, YouTube. https://goo.gl/wTtLOU
- "Your numbers — What's your communication grade level?" by Randall Bolten, LinkedIn. https://goo.gl/Zpw5Y7
- "How accountants can give awesome financial presentations," Sageworks blog. https://goo.gl/SOgvA6

Share Your Expertise: Why It Pays And How To Do It

Tax lawyer Kelly Phillips Erb, aka "taxgirl," has written for The New York Times and is now a staff writer for Forbes.com, but she never set out to be a famous blogger or national thought leader.

She became those, however, by sharing what she knows. And along the way, she's gained trust (and business) from clients, prospects and peers. Erb, whose blog ranks No. 5 on WalletHub's Best Tax Blogs, has good advice for anyone considering writing as part of their marketing or business development efforts. Even if you don't like to write, her tips can help you share your expertise in other ways (e.g., videos, podcasts).

Why it pays to generate thought leadership content

- Credibility
- Relatability
- Networking

Providing "thought leadership," or sharing your expertise without necessarily charging for it, is one way to establish yourself as an essential advisor to clients and prospects. It can create trust and boost credibility.

What started as an effort to educate existing clients became a showcase of Erb's expertise and a way to connect with future clients, too. "If you establish yourself as an authority, it allows you to stand out in a really competitive market," she says. "It's a really great way to get noticed."

Erb found that posting tax law articles on the Internet leveled the playing field relative to much larger firms, especially when she and her husband formed their own law firm in 2000. "We didn't have $5,000 to update the website or place ads in Pennsylvania Lawyer magazine," she says. "'One of the great things about writing …is [that] you don't have to put huge dollars behind it."

Another benefit of content marketing is that clients see her as human and likeable—key traits for winning trust. "Writing helps people put a face to you," she says. "My readers know I am a mom and have three kids. I talk all the time about how I'm a busy mom."

Showing that you're relatable is important for many service professionals, Erb explains: "Especially with CPAs and attorneys, people aren't coming to you because it's a great moment for them. It's usually because something bad has happened, or they're worried something bad might happen or they're overwhelmed. They're coming to you because there's a problem. When those people are looking for who can help them, they want a human."

Kelly Phillips Erb
JD/LLM, Taxation

Kelly Phillips Erb is a founding shareholder of The Erb Law Firm, PC, and a senior editor at Forbes.com, where she writes the popular taxgirl blog, which has been recognized by the American Bar Association Journal as one of the top 100 blogs written by lawyers and named to the ABA Journal Blawg Hall of Fame. She has served numerous positions with the Pennsylvania Bar Association, has been tapped by numerous national media outlets to explain taxes in plain English, and is the author of Ask the Taxgirl: Everything Parents Should Know about Filing Taxes and Home, Sweet Rental: Busting the Hype of Homeownership. Erb has both her JD and LLM in taxation from Temple University School of Law.

  @taxgirl

#NextLevelFirm

Finally, Erb's writing has led to strong networking with industry peers and with other important audiences. She first realized this when her blog was named in 2008 to the best legal blogs by the American Bar Association's ABA Journal, and again when asked to speak to tax professors at a law symposium. "I realized that new media had the potential to affect not only my relationships with clients but also other professionals and colleagues."

How to become a thought leader

- ✓ Define goals
- ✓ Don't overcommit
- ✓ Find your lane
- ✓ Get a system

If you want to write and develop thought leadership content, Erb has several tips.

First, define you goals. "What is it you hope to accomplish?" she asks. If you need the phone to ring immediately, an online equivalent of a Yellow Page ad might be more helpful. Writing articles for your company blog or newsletter is a longer-term play that can establish you as a resource, get you noticed and showcase your expertise when your firm shows up in Internet searches.

Second, don't overcommit. A common mistake new writers make is to set expectations on the blog that articles will be posted daily or more regularly than schedules allow. "Don't be afraid to know your limitations," Erb says. Pacing yourself is also part of providing thought leadership content.

"Everything doesn't have to be a journal article," she says. One friend offers brief advice each week on Facebook in the form of a post titled Tax Tip Tuesday. You could create a brief list, or tell a story of a recent meeting that helps clients and prospects learn from others' circumstances. Answering questions from readers once you've started to cultivate a following can generate terrific blog posts as well.

Another way to limit any burden is to line up guest columns or interview another professional who has expertise outside your realm. "Not only are you networking and possibly helping someone else with their business, which is a good thing because they might be happy to refer someone back to you, you're also reminding people, 'Hey, this is what I do.'"

Third, find your voice and your medium of communication. Don't assume you have to write about everything related to accounting. Sometimes focusing on a niche is better than taking a broad approach to your writing. "If you only like to do sales tax, write about sales tax and become the authority on sales tax, and when ABC News is looking for an expert on sales tax, they'll come to you," Erb says. And if you're not enthusiastic about writing articles, look for other ways to share your expertise: Facebook entries, brief videos on YouTube or podcasts addressing popular topics among your customers. "There are so many ways to put your 2 cents in," she says.

> " If you establish yourself as an authority, it allows you to stand out in a really competitive market. It's a really great way to get noticed. "

#NextLevelFirm

Finally, work out a system. Erb likes to keep a list of potential article topics in her purse so that whenever ideas strike, she can record them. You may need to set aside a block of time each day to write or develop ideas. Learn to edit your writing or ask others in your office to be a second set of eyes.

Erb is a strong proponent of sharing expertise via thought leadership, because the cumulative impact is that it builds your practice. "Whether you're blogging or doing a podcast or having a nice, updated website, it allows you to control how you present yourself to the potential client and gives the client the opportunity to understand you're a real person and you [realize] your job is to help them," she says.

RESOURCES

- Kelly Phillips Erb's blogs. https://kellyphillipserb.wordpress.com/blogs/
- Articles by Kelly Phillips Erb. http://goo.gl/kgpygj
- "7 Ways accountants can 'do' thought leadership and content marketing," Sageworks blog. http://goo.gl/ICo0up

Take These 5 Steps Toward Better Pricing

When someone has a baby, do you want to know about the baby—boy or girl, name, what it looks like, health—or do you want details on how many hours labor lasted, which doctors were involved and how much the hospital bill is likely to be?

The baby is what is important, not what it took to get the baby here.

Similarly, accountants who base pricing on a timesheet are like a parent who is fixated on the hospital bill and staff rather than the details of their newborn child. Clients are eager to hear how an accounting firm can meet their overall needs and help them grow their business, according to Ronald J. Baker, the accounting industry's longtime crusader against the billable hour. They're not as interested in how many hours the engagement will take or what documents will be produced as a result.

Essentially, the billable hour measures the wrong thing, says Baker, author of seven best-selling books and founder of VeraSage Institute, a think tank dedicated to teaching value pricing to professionals and improving the professions for posterity. "The hourly method focuses on inputs, efforts and activity at the expense of value, results and outcomes for the customer."

Therefore, while pricing based on the billable hour can be profitable, it is not optimal. "There are thousands of [firms] around the world across all professional sectors—law, advertising, consulting, IT—that have completely moved away from the billable hour," Baker says. "They have happier team members, they have better quality of life, and they have happier customers and more loyal customers, because they're creating more value for them."

For firms interested in improving their pricing method, a major challenge in moving away from billable hours can be identifying and describing exactly what is valuable—from the client's point of view—about the professional's work and then putting a number on that value. Pricing based on value is customer-centric—a major shift from hour-based pricing of services.

Baker says that the subjective nature of value is not the only thing that makes value pricing challenging. Value is also related to context, so it can vary. "Value changes, and it changes based on time, place, location and what outcome customers are seeking," he says. For example, Baker notes, a bottle of water may be worth dramatically different amounts to different people, depending on their point of view and context: Is the person in a desert? Washing a dog? Standing in a flooded basement? Similarly, a can of Coke or an airline seat may be worth different amounts to different people at different times.

Ronald J. Baker

Ronald J. Baker started his CPA career in 1984 with KPMG's Private Business Advisory Services in San Francisco. Today, he is the founder of VeraSage Institute—the leading think tank dedicated to educating professionals internationally. He is also a radio talk-show host on the www.VoiceAmerica.com show: The Soul of Enterprise: Business in the Knowledge Economy, and the best-selling author of seven books, including Implementing Value Pricing.

  @ronaldbaker

> **" The hourly method focuses on inputs, efforts and activity at the expense of value, results and outcomes for the customer. "**

> **Value changes** based on time, place, location and what outcome customers are seeking.

"It is customer value that determines all prices in a free market or in any market, so we need to start with value to the customer and work backward," he says.

So how does an accounting firm begin to take steps toward achieving optimal pricing? Here are a few of Baker's tips:

DIP YOUR TOE IN THE WATER

"I'm not asking people to cannonball into the pool and do this via a letter to all customers saying, we're going to switch to this," Baker says. Instead, decide to try a new approach with one customer. It could be a new customer or an existing one. "I started my firm with older customers, existing relationships, because I felt I could talk with them candidly," he says. "It doesn't really matter where you start." Baker says he has seen firms move from billable hours to fixed-price agreements with 100 percent of customers in as few as three months or more commonly in 18 months.

START THE "VALUE" CONVERSATION WITH CLIENTS

"The customer could care less about costs, so I don't want to have a conversation about something they don't care about—my efforts, my hours—and I don't want to have a conversation about something they're trying to lower—my price," Baker says. "But I do want to have a conversation with them about something they're trying to maximize, which is value."

Instead of focusing client pricing conversations on discussions of scope of work and deliverables, try establishing the idea that *value* is what's important. Baker recommends saying something like, "Mr. Customer, we will only undertake this engagement if we can agree, to our mutual satisfaction, that the value we are creating is greater than the price we are charging you. Is that acceptable?"

LISTEN AND THEN DIAGNOSE/PRESCRIBE

Since the customer's view of value is subjective and based on context, figure out whether—to continue Baker's metaphor from above—the client is in the desert, washing the dog or in the basement in order to identify what is of value and how you can help. "Every customer's different, so you have to start by asking the customer what it is they're trying to achieve and comprehend it at a real deep level," Baker says.

Take These 5 Steps Toward Better Pricing

#NextLevelFirm

Questions to diagnose your client's needs:

✓ *What do you expect from us?*

✓ *How do you see us helping you address your challenges and opportunities?*

✓ *How do you define a successful relationship with your CPA?*

✓ *What is your definition of success?*

✓ *What growth plans do you have?*

✓ *What are your future plans?*

✓ *Tell me 10 things you would never hear people say about your industry.*
   (*This is to generate ideas for how the client can be different from its peers.*)

✓ *What advice would you give to someone who wanted to enter your industry?*

CHANGE THE LANGUAGE

Once you understand the client's needs, be careful how you talk about what your firm will do. Instead of talking about efforts and hours, talk about outcomes that are customized to your client, based on what you understand them to value. In describing what your firm can provide, consider not only the materialistic value that can be measured (tax savings, reduction of risk, reduction of expenses, increases in productivity), but also what Baker calls the "spiritual value" that you can provide. "Talk about your social relationships, your networks—that you can help the customer do other things because you're connected to the community. You know insurance agents, lawyers, real estate agents. In fact, anything they need, there's probably someone in the firm's network that can help them. Clients love to tap into our networks because they know how big they are."

PRICE THE CUSTOMER, NOT THE SERVICE

As part of shifting to a new pricing model, Baker recommends developing a "value council," a group of people who can grow into being the experts at pricing. The value council will also help develop options—a range of prices for a range of services or outcomes—similar to the Green, Gold and Platinum choices offered by American Express. "Firms need to get over the idea that there's one optimal price for customers. We walk around with an acceptable range of prices that we're willing to pay for something, whether it's CPA services or a can of Coke," he says.

Instead of talking about efforts and hours, **talk about outcomes that are customized to your client,** based on what you understand them to value.

#NextLevelFirm

Look for people to serve on the value council who are confident that the company's services are worth every penny and who can learn from reading and from others about what might work and what doesn't. Members of the value council don't have to be partners or even staff members. "In fact, I think it's better to have someone on the council like a receptionist who might not know the technical aspects but who knows the customers really well and might bring valuable insights into the customer," he says. Someone like that "just might be braver to price, like a spouse usually is. Spouses are braver because they have to live with the consequences of a CPA underselling themselves."

RESOURCES

- "The firm of the future," by Ronald J. Baker, Journal of Accountancy. http://goo.gl/u3eJ9h
- "Pricing on purpose," by Ronald J. Baker, Journal of Accountancy. http://goo.gl/UE1xvU
- "A tale of two theories," by Ronald J. Baker, LinkedIn. https://goo.gl/4BCiTc
- "The first law of marketing: All value is subjective," by Ronald J. Baker, LinkedIn. https://goo.gl/QaZDtY
- "The second law of marketing: All prices are contextual," by Ronald J. Baker, LinkedIn. https://goo.gl/lix4dP
- "Who is in charge of value at your accounting firm?" Sageworks blog. https://goo.gl/1rLQs4

Create Time and Capacity for Advisory Services

Every time Tom Hood, who is executive director and CEO of the Maryland Association of CPAs, gives a speech (and he gives a *lot* of speeches), he asks his audiences of accountants about the top challenges they face.

Invariably, Hood says, the top challenges get boiled down to:

- Not having enough time
- Doing more with less
- Information overload and
- Keeping up with change

Accountants "are basically just heads down, trying to keep up with the day to day," says Hood, one of Accounting Today's 100 Most Influential People in Accounting and one of LinkedIn's Top 150 Influencers. They don't have any time to think, much less take on a new project.

But the more Hood talked with accountants who made a shift to being proactive and offering innovative services, the more he realized that these individuals had something in common: "They were actually creating time in their very busy lives to figure out some of the new things," he says. These accountants understand that "time is never going to come to you; no one's going to give it to you. You're going to have to create it."

How do you do that, though?

HERE ARE HOOD'S SIX SUGGESTIONS

1 | Use the latest and most efficient technologies

Accountants who are making time are doing so using technology to solve their business problems, Hood says. "That goes for everything from workflow, business process re-engineering—all of those kinds of things—to implementing cloud technologies to make things more efficient."

2 | Make your workflow and processes efficient

Hood recommends examining what is being done, why and whether it's essential. If someone is producing a report, figure out who it goes to and determine how they use it. "Is this business process accomplishing what we intend it to at the costs we intend? Oftentimes in a period of fast change,

Tom Hood
CPA

Tom Hood is executive director and CEO of the Maryland Association of CPAs, one of Accounting Today's 100 Most Influential People in Accounting and one of LinkedIn's Top 150 Influencers. He is also founder and CEO of the Business Learning Institute, which provides customized, competency-based curriculum and education for the finance and accounting profession. He has held numerous positions within state and national CPA organizations and is a frequent keynote speaker at industry conferences.

 *@tomhood*

> " Time is never going to come to you; no one's going to give it to you. You're going to have to create it. "

#NextLevelFirm

people change, roles change, and we don't have time to look out for that," he notes. "If you can make a little time to do that and cut out the things that are unnecessary, you can reinvest that time you just created into looking at new technology that might save you even more time."

3 | Engage your people

Despite recent talk about how workers from the millennial generation crave work that matters, Hood stresses that all workers want this, not just young professionals. "Our profession, left to its own devices, can put [workers] through the rigors of 'paying your dues,' which is often mind-numbing work that doesn't feel like it has a purpose," he says. Involve staff in the strategy of the firm and in projects that might impact them. Connect them with work that matters. You will find workers more engaged and more willing to put in discretionary effort, Hood predicts. "That means they're the people that will walk through walls for you," he says. "How much more would they get done because they care? You just created a ton of capacity that you can reinvest in learning the new skills that are needed to become a proactive business advisor."

> " How much more would they get done because they care? You just created a ton of capacity that you can reinvest in learning the new skills that are needed to become a **proactive business advisor.** "

4 | Maximize the software and tools you have

A lot of firms aren't really training their staff on the core technology they already have, so existing technology and workflow processes aren't maximized. "If you're not training people on what you have, it's like giving someone a Ferrari and then they drive it around like it's a go cart," Hood says. Look for ways to get the most out of your current technology and tools. For example, a 20-minute training session on how to create tables in Excel may result in better, faster analysis.

5 | Focus on your best "A" clients

Agree on what being one of the firm's best clients means, then rank clients as A or B clients. Look at size and profit, but also consider whether the client generates the kind of work that fits the firm's values and that challenges staff and helps them grow. Consider whether the client is difficult to deal with because they cause delays or extra costs. Then, Hood suggests, consider raising your prices on the B clients by a minimum of 30 percent. "Say, 'You're

tough to deal with; we love you but you're never ready when we are' or whatever the issues are, then say you're going to have to raise the price 30 percent or more," Hood recommends. "Half of those clients will say "see you" and the other half will take it. "Not only will you create more time for proactive services for the A clients, but more money comes in and people feel better."

6 | Communicate your services/cross-sell

If staff understand that they are not just generating fees from clients but they are actually making an impact on that customer, they will look for opportunities to communicate how they can save the client money or help the client make improvements in their business. This opens doors for cross-selling, making each client more valuable.

Hood says even the busiest of firms can take steps to create time, which they can then use on proactive, future-focused activities. "It's all about the little things," he says. "Just make little pieces of time and then make sure you're reinvesting that time savings into the next thing that will save even more time. You have to be disciplined so you don't squander that time."

RESOURCES

- "Why accountants must learn to ride these big waves of change," by Tom Hood, LinkedIn. https://goo.gl/zdbKI3
- Are you leading the transformation of finance and accounting?" by Tom Hood, LinkedIn. https://goo.gl/kqEuJh
- CPA Success Blog, hosted by The Business Learning Institute. http://blionline.org/blog/
- "Time savings—just when you need it," Sageworks blog. http://goo.gl/3vbhJi

Motivating Partners to Develop a Firm of Trusted Advisors

> "The real successful model of a CPA firm is one that's proactive, that can satisfy the client's needs—maybe in ways that they don't know."

How can a CPA firm differentiate itself?

Is it by having lots of expertise? No; many firms have expertise in accounting matters.

Is it by the years of experience of their partners and staff? No; many firms have people with decades of experience.

Is it by providing quality accounting and tax work? No; lots of firms provide accounting and tax work that satisfies their clients.

CPA firms routinely struggle to describe how they legitimately stand out from competitors, according to Marc Rosenberg, a nationally recognized consultant on CPA firm management and partner issues and a perennial pick for *Accounting Today's* list of the Top 100 Most Influential People in Accounting. But the answer to differentiation is actually straightforward, he says.

"The real successful model of a CPA firm is one that's proactive, that can satisfy the client's needs—maybe in ways that they don't know," says Rosenberg, who is also founder of The Rosenberg Survey, the most authoritative annual survey of mid-sized CPA firm performance statistics in the U.S. "Accounting is all about people—listening and providing and being with your clients and inspiring and mentoring your staff to figure out what clients want and delivering it—and then some. Accounting is just a tool to get to what clients really need: advice on all affairs directly and indirectly related to financial."

Rosenberg says that many firms buy into the idea of accountants being proactive advisors; many construct strategic plans to develop such a firm, but they fall short on execution. "They might devote part of a retreat to it once a year. They might even come up with a document, but they don't have a clue how to implement it."

Other firms may say, "We partners all got together and decided this is what we want: to be trusted advisors to our clients." But as long as each partner is individually left to determine to what degree he or she will be a trusted advisor and how to become one, that strategy goes nowhere, Rosenberg says.

Marc Rosenberg
CPA

Marc Rosenberg is a nationally known consultant, author and speaker on CPA firm management, strategy and partner issues. He has been one of Accounting Today's Top 100 Most Influential People in Accounting for 12 consecutive years, and is among 10 named to INSIDE Public Accounting's 2015 Most Recommended Consultants. Rosenberg is the author of a series on CPA firm practice management.

His 12 books include Partner Compensation, Mergers, Partner Buy-Out Plans, How to Bring in New Partners, Firm Management & Governance, Succession Planning and Retreats.

@mrosenbergcpa

Rosenberg says there are three requirements to moving beyond the strategic plan and actually becoming a firm of trusted advisors:

- ✓ Discipline
- ✓ Accountability and
- ✓ Management

DISCIPLINE

When each partner averages 1,100 to 1,500 billable hours per year securing clients, meeting with clients, getting the clients' work done and overseeing work being done for clients, they find little time to actually manage their firms and nurture the staff. But Rosenberg says active management is critical to developing a firm of trusted advisors. Delegating duties to others and sticking with the delegation requires discipline. "Well managed firms hate to see their partners doing work that could be done by a staff person," he says. "Walking the talk is the magic answer. You know that's the right answer, but what are you doing to make it happen?"

Discipline is also required to develop leaders through mentoring programs to ensure that staff rise to become partners and ultimately become ready and capable of taking over the clients of older partners as they get close to retirement. Rosenberg points out that failing to do this is part of what has caused the recent merger frenzy in the accounting industry. "The vast majority of the firms that are merging up into bigger firms do so because over a period of many years, they were unable to develop staff into partners to succeed them and are thus unable to keep the firm going," he says. "Eighty percent of all CPA firms fail to reach the second generation, and we're not just talking about sole practitioners."

ACCOUNTABILITY

To develop a firm of trusted advisors, Rosenberg says, everyone—including partners—has to be held accountable for their role in becoming consultants. "If there are no consequences to failing to achieve a goal or an expectation, then it's less likely that the goal or expectation will be accomplished," he says. "There's a reason why the top 100 firms are the top 100 firms. They get it when it comes to things like partner accountability."

Rosenberg once worked with a firm where a partner had been a partner for 30 years but was committing numerous transgressions against the firm. "He was late collecting his receivables, he was late billing clients, he was abusive to staff, his client base was shrinking, nobody knew where he was during the day," Rosenberg says. "At the group meeting, of seven or eight partners… I started out by saying, 'I don't know what's worse, the fact that he has committed all of these transgressions or that all the rest of you let him.'"

"Partners really have a tough time holding partners accountable," says Rosenberg. It's the firms below the top 100 that struggle mightily with accountability."

> " Accounting is just a tool to get to what clients really need: advice on all affairs directly and indirectly related to financial. "

> " **Eighty percent of all CPA firms fail to reach the second generation**, and we're not just talking about sole practitioners. "

#NextLevelFirm

Motivating Partners to Develop a Firm of Trusted Advisors

MANAGEMENT

Intervention and coaching by management is necessary for helping personnel at all levels to achieve the firm's core values. "The real thing you need is a managing partner or a management group that really takes their role seriously in managing the performance and behavior of other partners," Rosenberg says. "It's not hitting them over the head—'Did you do the goal? Did you do the goal?' but it's 'How are you doing, and how can I help you?' "

Good managers will also set firm-wide goals that will incentivize and nudge their partners to offer advisory services and to develop staff appropriately, and these goals should be tied to partner compensation. "Don't just allocate income strictly based on hard-core production statistics. Those are important and they should be a big factor, but we've got to look at other things. We can't just talk about them. You have to have specific goals."

Achieving accountability can be difficult, but finding a way to hold partners responsible ensures that partners meet their own goals and that the partners' goals will mesh well with the firm's overall objectives. Rosenberg says firms have many means available to achieve partner accountability. Below are 10, in order of usage by firms but not necessarily in order of the most effective, according to Rosenberg:

1 | Compensation

2 | Meeting with the managing partner for some "behavior modification"

3 | Upward evaluations of the partners by the staff

4 | Peer pressure

5 | Partner evaluations

6 | Partner goal setting

7 | Client satisfaction surveys

8 | Living and breathing the firm's core values

9 | Clarifying the roles and expectations of each partner, "with crystal clarity"

10 | The "door" (i.e., termination)

RESOURCES

- *CPA Firm Management & Governance* by Marc Rosenberg, Rosenberg Associates website. http://goo.gl/ZWZOQv
- *Strategic Planning and Goal Setting for Results* by Marc Rosenberg, Rosenberg Associates website. http://goo.gl/DBqEmV
- *CPA Firm Retreats: The Do-It-Yourself Guide* by Marc Rosenberg, Rosenberg Associates website. http://goo.gl/mBIlcl
- The Marc Rosenberg blog on firm website. http://rosenbergassoc.com/marcs-blog/
- "Top mistakes accountants are making with their clients," Sageworks blog. http://goo.gl/bZBvOu

A Compensation Plan That Breeds Trusted Advisors

If you're looking for a compensation system that will keep partners engaged, grow the firm and develop trusted advisors, look no further.

Seriously, look no further, says August J. Aquila, a consultant specializing in professional service firm compensation plans and mergers and the author of *Leadership at its Strongest: What Successful Managing Partners Do* and *Compensation as a Strategic Asset*.

Compensation alone won't motivate partners to accomplish all of these goals, according to Aquila. Instead, it's the firm's culture that will:

- define values and behaviors expected of partners and then
- reward partners whose behavior meets expectations and advances those values.

"If we think compensation in and of itself is going to make someone a trusted advisor, we sort of have the tail wagging the dog," Aquila says. "The firm's culture is the dog, and the tail is the compensation."

In other words, to keep partners engaged, motivate them to grow the firm and to develop as trusted advisors, the firm must first identify its driving values, and then describe the behaviors that will support those principles. For example, perhaps the firm believes that teamwork can provide clients with better service, allowing one staff member to identify a client's needs that another partner might miss. Therefore, tying compensation with behavior that boosts client teamwork and with the behavior's beneficial results can motivate partners to achieve the firm's goals more quickly.

"When you think of the firm's compensation, most firms have historically put the emphasis on performance—meaning production, typically: billable hours, business development," Aquila says. "There hasn't been equal emphasis on behavior."

This can result in the following kind of partner, Aquila says: "I'm a prima donna, I'm a pain in the ass, but I bring in a lot of business, but I turn off staff, which means we have to spend more on recruiting, and it's sort of a vicious circle."

"Somewhere along the line, firms have to decide: Do they want this individual or don't they want this individual? No matter what compensation plan you have, it's not going to make any difference" in that type of situation, he says.

Similarly, the firm has hard choices even before beginning a discussion about compensation systems if they have, as Aquila puts it, "someone who

August J. Aquila
MBA, PhD

August J. Aquila consults with professional service firms around the world in the areas of compensation design, mergers & acquisitions, partnership issues and strategic planning.

He has been named one of Accounting Today's Top 100 Most Influential People in Accounting and was named to the Association for Accounting Marketing's Hall of Fame in 2003. Follow him on Linked-In, email him at aaquila@aquilaadvisors.com or find more articles at www.aquilaadvisors.com.

   *@AquilaAdvisors*

was a solid performer 10 or 15 years ago but has [unofficially] retired and hasn't told anyone."

"Under a new compensation program, it's really important to look at each partner in the firm and make a decision: A, are they good 'citizens,' and B, do they perform or can they perform at the level you want them to?"

Once those questions are answered and the firm's values are linked to desired behavior, firms can then develop a compensation plan using metrics that focus partners on developing some of the "soft skills" that can build them into trusted advisors.

"The trusted advisor, when you think about it, isn't necessarily trusted because of their technical skills," Aquila says. "Their technical skills are important, but the trusted advisor is trusted because of the way they behave, act and communicate, which goes back to soft skills. I can be the best tax consultant in the world, but if I cannot communicate that to a client or cannot have empathy with a client or cannot show the client how I'm helping them, do I really become a trusted advisor?"

Aquila says being a trusted advisor is about having the client's best interests in mind. He recalls one firm that actually told a client another CPA firm in the market would be better for helping with a particular problem. "Most firms would say, I can do it, whether they could or not and then they'd try to figure out how to do it and maybe do a so-so job," he says. "This one firm said, 'Look, we're not good in this one area and we think this other firm could help you a lot better.' That turned out to be a client for life for the first firm."

Compensation should be planned in such a way that it encourages partners to act in the client's best interest. Total compensation structures vary from firm to firm, of course, but Aquila suggests that base salary should make up roughly 70 percent of total compensation in a healthy pay package. Bonus would be about 25 percent, and a payment for return on capital invested in the firm could be the remaining 5 percent. For each type of compensation, goals and metrics measuring achievement against those goals could be categorized into three buckets:

- **economics**
- **business development**
- **value enhancement**

Each bucket could have metrics aimed at measuring both performance and the behavior, he says.

> "The trusted advisor is trusted because of **the way they behave, act and communicate,** which goes back to soft skills."

> "Compensation should be planned in such a way that it encourages partners to act in the client's best interest."

A Compensation Plan That Breeds Trusted Advisors

#NextLevelFirm

THE ECONOMICS BUCKET

The economics bucket covers metrics that measure revenue generation for the firm. Aquila encourages using cash collected as a metric here, because it is less easily manipulated as a performance index than, say, chargeable hours or billable hours. Another metric could be realization or gross profitability of clients.

THE BUSINESS DEVELOPMENT BUCKET

The business development bucket could include performance metrics related to new business (that the partner brings in for themselves or brings in for the firm) and cross-selling (the opportunities created for the partner or for others). Behavior-focused metrics could be related to arranging meetings between potential prospects and partners.

THE VALUE ENHANCEMENT BUCKET

The value enhancement bucket covers behavior and performance that enhance the value of the entire company, Aquila says. Example metrics could include tracking the number of seminars that a partner gave in support of efforts to become a go-to expert in the market on a particular subject. Another might be using staff and client surveys to determine whether the partner always puts the client first, if that is a firm value. "Measure [value enhancement] in a simple way, asking your staff or clients, 'Do you feel that Partner A puts clients first?' and using answers like always, sometimes or needs improvement."

Some parts of the compensation package might place more emphasis on behavior or performance metrics aimed at value enhancement. Others could focus more on firm economics or business development, Aquila says.

Ultimately, activities should be driven by the firm's vision and the firm's leaders, Aquila says. "If the firm doesn't have that, if the firm doesn't really know what it wants to achieve or how to achieve it, then people come in and they just behave any way they want to."

RESOURCES

- *Compensation as a Strategic Asset: The New Paradigm*, by August J. Aquila and Coral L. Rice (AICPA 2007). http://goo.gl/zSuZNQ
- *Leadership at Its Strongest: What Successful Managing Partners Do*, by Robert J. Lees, August J. Aquila and Derek Klyhn (Bay Street Group, LLC, 2013). http://goo.gl/fBKFQr
- *How to Engage Partners in the Firm's Future*, by August J. Aquila and Robert J. Lees (Bay Street Group, LLC, 2013). https://goo.gl/QW2M1k
- Articles by August J. Aquila on LinkedIn. https://goo.gl/v2Kxzy
- "Want to discourage price shopping by your accounting clients? Here's how," Sageworks blog. https://goo.gl/MMahK1

#NextLevelFirm

Retaining Clients During a Firm Transition

Imagine a partner announces their retirement and your firm buys out the equity stake. Five years later, the partner is still working with and controlling the same client relationships as always. Worse yet, the "retired" partner is getting more and more difficult to work with every day but has been fully paid. What do you do? Or imagine the partner actually does retire, but his or her clients leave the firm, too.

Terrence E. Putney, CEO of Transition Advisors LLC and co-author of the book, *CPA Firm Mergers & Acquisitions: How to Buy a Firm, How to Sell a Firm, and How to Make the Best Deal*, says this scenario has happened and will happen again without proper planning to manage the transition of partners and their client relationships.

Nothing can turn a good purchase of an accounting firm or the buyout of a partner into a bad deal faster than the loss of clients after the transaction closes, says Putney, who also is former Managing Director – Mergers and Acquisitions for RSM McGladrey. Client loss can wreck the value of the deal and hurt the firm's reputation as trusted advisors. During transitions—as it should be throughout the life of the accounting firm—it's all about the client.

"If you're a trusted advisor, then the client depends on you for unique insights, but if you're no longer going to be available, which is eventually going to happen to all of us, then helping the client transition that dependence they have on you as a trusted advisor to a different trusted advisor you have personally chosen as your successor can create value," Putney says.

Having a deal structure and a business plan in place that encourages a strong transition of clients to the successor firm can make all the difference between a smooth changeover and a nightmare. "You have to understand how to treat clients in a transition like this so they want to stay with the successor firm," Putney advises.

Every deal should be structured to motivate parties to execute the client retention plan, he says. And the business plan should recognize that client relationships are often very personal—for both the client and the accountant. Practically speaking, this means incorporating sufficient time for a transition. "As a rule of thumb, we recommend two years for a proper transition to be executed, but it depends on the kinds of clients and kinds of services and how often the client interacts with the firm," Putney says. A 90-day transition (which Putney sees quite often) is not at all sufficient to respect the client's needs, he adds.

Terrence E. Putney
CPA

Terrence E. Putney is CEO of Transition Advisors, LLC, a national consulting firm to the CPA profession providing services related to transition of CPA firm ownership. During his 38 years in the profession, Putney has been the managing partner of a mid-sized CPA firm and Managing Director–M&A for RSM McGladrey.

He is widely published in numerous trade publications, including the Journal of Accountancy, and is a frequent speaker for professional conferences on the subject of owner transition and succession. He is the immediate past-president of the CPA Consultants' Alliance and can be reached at tputney@transitionadvisors.com.

  @PutneyTerry

> **" As a rule of thumb, we recommend two years for a proper transition to be executed**, but it depends on the kinds of clients and kinds of services and how often the client interacts with the firm. "

The deal structure and business plan should take into account whether a client is "firm loyal" or "partner loyal." The larger the firm or the client, the more likely that the client is not as attached to an individual as to the firm. In other cases, clients have developed close, personal relationships with the individual, so it can be like losing a friend when the partner leaves, Putney says.

"If you treat it like 'It's no big deal, we're going to keep doing the same work and why should the client care?' you're potentially at risk for the client to say, 'I don't know you guys. I've worked with this guy for 20 years. Who are you?'"

Putney says business plans should ensure that the person who has had the relationship with the client is actively involved in the transition. "It's difficult to go to someone you've worked for 20 years and say I'm no longer your accountant. If the seller's not motivated to properly participate, it doesn't work."

Active involvement doesn't mean holding on, he adds. "That means giving it up slowly, backing themselves up into the background."

But it also requires the seller to continue to be present, for a time. "If [the seller] is not there that's a real problem. Or if they're totally checked out that's a problem as well."

Putney recommends a written plan so that all parties understand how the transition is going to work and can hold each other accountable.

Deals can be structured in a number of ways to ensure client retention, including the following:

- ✓ The agreement can include an adjustment that amends the deal price based on client retention.
- ✓ It could establish a fixed price after at least two years.
- ✓ In mergers, where selling partners become owners in the buying firm and where the price is based on how much business is being brought in, there might be look-back adjustments to ownership if a certain amount of drop-off in the client book occurs.

A retiring partner selling to other partners doesn't generally pose as high of a risk for losing clients as in an external sale, but you still want to ensure a proper transition, Putney says. One common approach is requiring two years' notice of retirement. When the transition of the client relationship must

#NextLevelFirm

Retaining Clients During a Firm Transition | 25

occur during that period, the client will have adjusted by the time the partner leaves, and the departure will be a non-event.

"One thing we have been adding into agreements is a requirement that [retiring partners] execute a written transition plan, and if they fail to execute…the deal is treated as if they've not given notice," Putney says. Typical consequences include either putting the deal on a contingent basis post-retirement (so any harm done is reflected in payments to retiring partners) or setting a discount (typically in the 20 to 30 percent range but sometimes as high as 50 percent) to compensate for the damage from failing to provide notice and execute the transition plan.

"When you've been doing this for 40 years or 45 years, it's just part of who you are, and these relationships are part of who you are," Putney says. "Walking away is really hard for some people to do. They can't bring themselves into have those conversations with the client."

"I've had guys in their 80s tell me 'My client doesn't want me to leave.' The reality is if you went to the client they'd say, 'I'm waiting for this guy to tell me when he's going to leave.'"

This is an important relationship to the client and their business, and they need to know who the successor's going to be, Putney says. "They don't want to find out by reading the obituaries one day that their accountant has passed and then it's, 'Who's my accountant now?'"

In M&A events, many firms tout the value of their partners to the practice, but the truth is that a tremendous amount of value is tied to a firm's ability to transition related clients. "One thing that sellers tell me often-times is, 'Nobody can replace me. I have these unique relationships with these clients. I go to their kids' weddings. They tell me things they wouldn't tell their spouse. It's taken me years to build that.' It's a very personal relationship with their clients," Putney says. "I respect that completely, but if you can't transition and put somebody else in place to take your place, your practice has no value."

> "One thing we have been adding into agreements is a requirement that [retiring partners] execute a **written transition plan**, and if they fail to execute…the deal is treated as if they've not given notice."

RESOURCES

- *CPA Firm Mergers & Acquisitions: How to Buy a Firm, How to Sell a Firm, and How to Make the Best Deal*, by Joel L. Sinkin and Terrence E. Putney, CPA. http://goo.gl/xVH8NU
- "CPA Firm Succession—Solidifying the Future," 12-part series by Joel Sinkin and Terrence E. Putney, CPA, July 2013–June 2014, Journal of Accountancy. http://goo.gl/YMT91x
- "Exit Strategies for Owners of CPA Firms," by Joel Sinkin and Terrence E. Putney, CPA, Pennsylvania CPA Journal, Summer 2015. http://goo.gl/se1z0B
- "3 Easy ways accountants can build on their clients' trust," Sageworks blog. http://goo.gl/KkiYDh

What Services Are Driving Our Industry Growth?

Ninety-percent of the accounting industry is tied to compliance services in areas such as accounting, audit and tax, but don't look there for encouraging signs of industry performance.

"If you look at those Level 1 services over the next decade, it's a slow death," says consultant Allan D. Koltin, who has been called the industry's biggest deal broker. "A Level 1 service is a service a client doesn't want but needs. A Level 2 service is a service a client both wants and needs, and hence, will pay value for."

He expects growth in Level 1 services to range from zero to no more than 3 percent in the next 10 years as technology continues to replace more of what accountants do when providing these types of services, and as clients look for the cheapest options because they need but don't want them. "You can't be in a business that only grows 0 to 3 percent, because your payroll and operating costs are going to grow much faster than that."

Instead, it will be services that involve advisory, consulting, wealth management and performing outsourcing functions (such as CFO duties) that offer the most opportunity for accounting firms during the next 10 years. These are the services offered by trusted advisors because it is these services that clients need and, more importantly, are willing to pay for, Koltin says.

HELPING WITH BUSINESS/FINANCIAL PROBLEMS— WHATEVER THEY MAY BE

To illustrate the point, consider Koltin's relationship with an accounting firm that serves Koltin's consultancy, based in Chicago's home of Cook County.

"There are 3,000 CPA firms in Cook County, and every one of them can do a financial statement or tax return," he says. Clients don't really want these services, but they need them in order to get a loan or comply with tax laws. "It's logical that I might as well take the cheapest one I can find, because it's a service I don't want but I have to have. We call this a commodity!"

But Koltin hasn't done that, because his CPA is a trusted advisor. "The partner on the account comes to my office once a month, and we spend 10 minutes talking about the financial statement. We spend the other 3 hours and 50 minutes talking about any business challenge or financial problem that I'm having in my business and sometimes in my personal life."

Allan D. Koltin
CPA, CMGA

Allan D. Koltin is the CEO of Koltin Consulting Group (KCG). KCG consults to CPA firms on strategy, growth, compensation, governance, profitability, talent, partner conflict/mediation and M&A/succession issues. Koltin is one of Accounting Today's Top 100 Most Influential People in Accounting, one of INSIDE Public Accounting's Most Recommended Consultants and a member of the CPA Practice Advisor Accounting Hall of Fame.

  @AllanDKoltin

"If you look at those Level 1 services over the next decade, it's a slow death."

#NextLevelFirm

> " What I like about this person and the firm is the mentality of 'We're in the business of helping our clients with their business and financial problems, whatever they may be.' "

"There's no audit checklist; there's no agreed-upon procedures. It's a blank pad of paper or iPad, and it's almost like a resident psychologist: 'Hey Allan, tell me how the month was. What's your game plan for the next month? What things that we've been talking about are continuing to be a problem, and how do we reach a decision to do something?' A lot of times we're not talking about accounting, taxes or audits—it's all business coaching and advice."

Instead, they're discussing service areas that may be underperforming, or discussing how to balance finite resources and finite time.

"So when another accounting firm calls me up and says they can do a cheaper audit or tax return, I'm not moving for $10,000; I'm probably not moving even if it's $20,000 less, because I value the trusted advisor relationship that I have with my CPA firm and I don't know that I can get that business coaching and advice elsewhere."

It is these types of relationships and services that represent the best revenue-growth opportunities for accounting firms.

LEVEL 2, 3 AND 4 SERVICES

Aside from Level 1, or compliance services, here's how Koltin sees growth rates breaking down over the next decade among the various levels of services provided by accounting firms:

Level 2 services: 5% to 10% growth

These are services that clients want and need and will pay value for—services that many firms can do in-house, such as estate planning and tax solutions (like helping with international tax, SALT and transfer pricing issues), business valuations, feasibility studies and budgeting.

Level 3 services: 10% to 20% growth

These include advisory work, consulting and outsourcing services, such as CFO work, and accounting firms often need to partner with a third-party expert or hire that expertise in house.

Level 4 services: 20% to 200% growth

These services focus on wealth management: helping the client accumulate, protect and grow their wealth. "The legendary story goes that a firm

resigned from the $100,000 audit so they could represent the client in the sale of their business," Koltin says. "The client gets $50 million, and $40 million of that gets parked with the CPA firm's asset management, and that annuity is worth five to 10 times what the audit was bringing in."

"Accounting firms are starting to get religion and understand that Level 1 is dying, and they're quickly migrating into Level 2, 3 and 4," Koltin says. "It reminds me of the old adage: If the railroad industry knew they were in the transportation business, they would still be around today." The railroad industry became entrenched in doing what they knew and what they always did, whereas the transportation industry offered more advanced forms of service that were valued by the customer, who became more willing to pay greater fees, Koltin says. Accounting firms that only do what they've always done and what they're most comfortable with—Level 1 services—will lose out to firms offering more advanced forms of services—Levels 2, 3 and 4— that are of more value to the client.

> "Accounting firms are starting to get religion and understand that **Level 1 is dying, and they're quickly migrating into Level 2, 3 and 4.**"

IMPACT ON DEAL-MAKING

The expected growth in Level 2, 3 and 4 services is also affecting industry consolidation, says Koltin, who in addition to his consultancy, also advises CPA firms on mergers and acquisitions.

About half of deal activity is related to succession activity or older partners looking to unlock goodwill value built up by the firm, but the other half is strategic.

Many firms are looking to build out product lines for the future but recognize that building those organically could take years and a lot of capital, accompanied by uncertainty and risk, so they choose to merge with a larger firm that already has the playbook. There's also a tremendous trend of local firms rolling up into regional firms, regional firms rolling up into mega-regionals, mega-regionals into nationals and nationals into global firms. As a result, Koltin expects industry consolidation to continue apace.

"Today, firms with no succession issues are doing upstream mergers because strategically, it makes sense," Koltin says. "They realize it's good for their people, partners and clients."

RESOURCES

- Multiple videos of Koltin providing advice and assessments on industry and management topics are available on the firm's website (http://goo.gl/o8pGfw), and various articles by Koltin about industry dynamics are also on the site (http://www.koltin.com/Knowledge/).
- "Growing your CPA practice," by Allan D. Koltin on National Life's Main Street Blog. https://goo.gl/KCyODZ
- "Stuck in compliance: The Grim Reaper of accounting firms," Sageworks blog. http://goo.gl/cVeLR7

#NextLevelFirm

Outside of M&A, How Will Your Firm Grow?

Consolidation is heating up in the accounting industry as firms seek scale and top rainmakers encounter a wave of partners looking to retire in a few years. Business combinations may provide growth opportunities for many firms, but what if your firm intends to forge ahead on its own? How will you grow?

Gale Crosley a consultant who consistently lands on *Accounting Today's* list of the Top 100 Most Influential People in Accounting, says that the old model of growing accounting firms isn't working well anymore. Growth traditionally came through "banker breakfasts" and "lawyer lunches," Crosley says, through a "boots on the ground" mentality about meeting with prospects and through a willingness to take virtually any kind of client. "Our old model was to be a generalist," Crosley says. "You'd hang out your shingle and do your accounting work for companies all over in town."

Today's more sophisticated and competitive accounting marketplace means these approaches aren't as productive, according to Crosley. Competition is tougher, and margins are tighter. In addition, traditional approaches fly in the face of the idea of being a trusted advisor. "You cannot be a student of an industry if you're working with 10 different industries," Crosley says.

Here are three ways Crosley believes firms can become trusted advisors and succeed in today's market: Be specialized, strategic and technology-centric.

DECLARE A MAJOR (SPECIALIZE)

Many firms have a book of business that "looks like alphabet soup" when it comes to the industries included, Crosley says. They may have some business clients that are veterinarians, some real estate agents, some not-for-profits and some tool-and-die makers. "That's a reflection of the past and where we are now," she says. In order to grow, firms need to move toward specialization.

"They need to declare a major they are going to go after," Crosley says. The "major" will be the industry that becomes the firm's specialty, making it easier to develop a reputation as dominant in that field. To identify your "major," Crosley recommends evaluating several industries. Interview thought leaders, competitors, other providers, prospects and clients in those markets, asking what issues are important along with other market-intelligence questions and trying to determine which industry

Gale Crosley
CPA

Gale Crosley, president at Crosley+Company, consults with accounting firms on revenue growth. She was the 2014 recipient of The Advisory Board's Hall of Fame Award. She has also been selected as one of the Most Recommended Consultants in INSIDE Public Accounting's Best of the Best Firms survey for 12 consecutive years, and as one of Accounting Today's Top 100 Most Influential People in Accounting for 10 consecutive years. She is an honors accounting graduate from the University of Akron, Ohio, winner of the Simonetti Distinguished Business Alumni Award and is an Editorial Advisor for the Journal of Accountancy.

@gcrosley

Be specialized, strategic and technology-centric.

#NextLevelFirm

has the best market conditions for your firm. Once you've narrowed that list of industries over a few months, select those worthy of your concerted efforts at mastering an understanding of the market dynamics and the needs of businesses. "Throw all your weight into those markets as it relates to growth," Crosley says. "Rather than just doing accounting work, you are stepping back and looking at the strategic aspects of the industry and not just year in and year out saying, 'Let's get the books closed or get the tax return out the door.'"

As your firm adds more industry-specific clients and current clients in that industry become more valuable, it becomes easier to grow in that market. And while your legacy "alphabet soup" book of business in various other industries may remain important, it will become less crucial to your future growth, and you'll find ways to taper it as desired.

BECOME A QUARTERBACK (BE STRATEGIC)

Another avenue for organic growth involves taking a more strategic approach to your clients. Under traditional growth models, most firms target one new client at a time and focus on what services or deliverables the firm can provide immediately—a tactical approach to client service. In this model, partners each have a book of business, and they're judged by how well they retain these clients and expand services to them.

Crosley recommends instead thinking more like a quarterback. Rather than trying to manage the client, the accountant's objective is to help the client identify and direct resources that can meet all of their needs.

"That means when you show up, you're not the answer man or answer lady; you become a resource manager for others you might want to bring into the fold," she says. "You start letting go of having to know answers for everything. It becomes a team sport."

> " When you show up, you're not the answer man or answer lady; you become a resource manager for others you might want to bring into the fold. You start letting go of having to know answers for everything. **It becomes a team sport.** "

USE TECHNOLOGY (GET TECHNOLOGY-CENTRIC)

Moving to a team-sport mentality is tough for accountants when they are driven by a business model that relies on hourly billings. "The billable hour model kills the ability to explore and discover and strategically put things together," Crosley says. "If you have a billable hour goal, you don't have any time to interview and learn and discover and look at strategy and growth."

Crosley believes that the new model for growth in the accounting industry involves tapping into the benefits of technology as a way to end reliance on billable hours and a way to provide partners with the opportunity to take a more active role in developing profitable service lines or industry niches that create value for clients. Technology also makes it easier for accountants to scale within their niches and to more efficiently find clients in a particular industry.

"It frees them up so they have the ability to do things that need to be done to become a trusted business advisor, and that grows the value of the firm more and more," she says.

> "If you have a billable hour goal, you don't have any time to interview and learn and discover and look at strategy and growth."

RESOURCES

- Crosley+Company Website. http://www.crosleycompany.com/
- "Is your growth model evolving and changing?" by Gale Crosley, CPA, Crosley website. http://goo.gl/k6Skb5
- *At the Crossroads: The Remarkable CPA Firm that Nearly Crashed, then Soared*, by Gale Crosley, CPA, and Debbie Stover (John Wiley & Sons, 2008). http://goo.gl/HOxpzt
- "4 Reasons to leverage technology in your accounting firm," infographic from Sageworks. http://web.sageworks.com/leverage-technology-infographic/

#NextLevelFirm

How to Develop a Growing Valuation Practice

Several years ago, a business owner called Tim McDaniel seeking a business valuation to support the sale of her business to her son. She claimed to know already the value of the business—$2.5 million—and simply needed McDaniel to prove that value to the bank for a loan backing the deal.

"I asked her, 'How'd you come up with that figure?' and she said, 'I belong to two country clubs, and that's how much I need to keep up the country club lifestyle,'" recalls McDaniel, principal and director of business valuations at Rea & Associates, and the author of Know and Grow The Value of Your Business: An Owners Guide to Retiring Rich.

The actual valuation showed the business was worth closer to $800,000, and while the owner was furious, the son understood that it would be difficult to repay a $2.5 million loan to the bank when the business was only making a couple of hundred thousand dollars a year, McDaniel says. At 65, however, the owner didn't have a lot of time to repair the situation so that she could generate the kind of money she wanted for retirement.

This client and experience taught McDaniel a lot about the importance of helping business owners understand their most valuable asset. And it holds a valuable lesson for anyone looking to develop a growing valuation practice: While the market for compliance-related valuations is static, opportunity abounds for valuation professionals to help business owners understand and grow the value of their biggest asset.

"It's important for the business owner to know five or six years before retirement what the actual value is and ways to maybe improve that value," McDaniel says. "We've been preaching a lot that your business is your biggest asset, so you should know what the value is. You shouldn't guess at it, and you should have a plan to increase its value."

Indeed, McDaniel's firm has a valuation product called "Know & Grow Valuation," which takes a plain-English approach to explaining valuations and helping owners develop strategies for maximizing business value. Selling valuations that are event driven (such as those related to death or divorce) is less challenging, but the Know & Grow Valuation projects are more enjoyable.

Tim McDaniel
CPA/ABV, ASA, CBA

Tim McDaniel is a principal of Rea & Associates, an Ohio public accounting firm, and is director of the firm's business valuations team. A recognized leader in the business valuation field, having been involved in more than 2,000 valuation engagements and numerous merger & acquisition transactions, he is the author of Know and Grow the Value of Your Business: An Owner's Guide to Retiring Rich and the author of Valuing and Selling Your Business: A Quick Guide to Cashing In.

  @GrowYourValue

> **Your business is your biggest asset, so you should know what the value is.** You shouldn't guess at it, and you should have a plan to increase its value.

"It's not driven by need; it's driven by their desire and wants," he says. "You're teaching owners about one of their most prized possessions outside of their families. They get to understand their business more and what it's worth."

In addition, these engagements sometimes feed into other consulting areas of the accounting firm, such as IT, risk management, internal controls, tax solutions and operations improvement.

McDaniel has the following tips for growing a valuation practice aimed at business owners:

1 | Have a solid "elevator pitch" ready

McDaniel recommends that you prepare to explain briefly the potential return on investment of a valuation. Among the areas where knowing the value of your business can be beneficial:

- Estate and personal planning
- Developing strategies to increase value
- Buy/sell agreements
- Assistance in determining the best exit strategy

2 | Develop a valuation product that is cost effective

"For business planning purposes in our marketplace, people aren't going to spend $10,000 to $15,000 for these kinds of valuations." McDaniel's "Know & Grow Valuation" product incorporates a more brief description of the business and the industry than a full-blown valuation for other purposes would include. "We don't spend a lot of time and effort writing about the things they already know, and this reduces the cost of the valuation." The valuation does, however, clearly explain all financial assumptions and all three valuation approaches in its calculation.

3 | Focus on face-to-face selling

McDaniel says he does a lot of public speaking and CPE classes, provides thought-leadership articles and has a lot of lunches with prospects and professionals outside his firm who may provide referrals.

4 | Train the firm's partners on the importance of valuation

"Your best sales force is internal," McDaniel says. "Make sure you engender the confidence of your partners that you're competent, and train everyone to recognize opportunities." Rea & Associates holds training to help others remember, for example, that if they're talking to a business owner, they should ask how many owners there are. If there is more than one, the accountant should ask to see the buy-sell agreement. "Most of these agreements are old, not updated and have terrible valuation provisions in them," he says, providing an opportunity for the firm to help.

> "You're teaching owners about one of their most prized possessions outside of their families. They get to understand their business more and what it's worth."

RESOURCES

- Rea & Associates Business Valuation Division website. http://www.knowandgrow.com/

- *Know and Grow the Value of Your Business: An Owner's Guide to Retiring Rich*, by Tim McDaniel (Apress 2013). http://goo.gl/ZaRLtr

- "Teach clients to treat their business like an investment," Sageworks blog. https://goo.gl/cDs8T1

Becoming a Future-Ready Firm

Accountants know all too well that tax prep services have become commoditized, with intense pricing pressure and clients who aren't firm-loyal. Is it possible to turn around the trend and differentiate your tax prep services?

"Absolutely," says Jody Padar, CEO/principal of Chicago-based public accounting firm New Vision CPA Group and author of The Radical CPA: New Rules for the Future-Ready Firm.

In addition, her approach to tackling this problem is the same approach that helps firms to offer more out of their trusted advisor status and to be ready for changes shaping business clients and their accounting firms.

"CPAs have traditionally been trusted advisors for the last 100 years," Padar says. "We just haven't had as much opportunity to really help because we were so busy doing the actual accounting and tax work."

Padar says new methods of offering services, providing services and pricing services afford accounting firms the opportunity and capacity to stall commoditization and develop more valued advisory relationships with clients. She illustrates these methods through an example of how a traditional firm might handle a tax return, compared with how her firm typically handles them.

A traditional firm might only see a client at tax time, when the client brings in a tangled mess of financial materials. As a result, "the firm charges the client $2,000 to put together essentially a set of books good enough to do the tax return," Padar says.

The client puts their copy of the return in a drawer and doesn't think about the accountant again until next February. Meanwhile, the firm has its staff working 12 hours a day starting in January to handle the compressed workload.

At Padar's firm, she says, someone seeking a business tax return in February or March will likely hear, "We don't do returns only. If you want to come into our practice, you have to at least connect with us four times a year."

Jody Padar
CPA, MST

Jody Padar is one of the accounting profession's foremost visionaries and pioneers. She is CEO and principal of the New Vision CPA Group, a public accounting firm based in the Chicago area. Jody is the author of The Radical CPA: New Rules for the Future-Ready Firm, a book that sparked a movement within the profession. She has been named numerous times to Accounting Today's Top 100 Most Influential People in Accounting.

  @jodypadarcpa

> " Traditional firms look at technology as a cost of doing business; they don't look at it as part of the process. "

A service package for those meetings and a tax return might sell for $6,000, and more frequent meetings with the client enable much of the work needed for preparing a return to be done by year end. "The client likes us because they're talking to us all year," Padar says. "I don't need any additional work [in February or March]. But if I can get you into my firm and I can talk to you four times a year and get to a place where we're doing year-end tax planning, then your return becomes a slam dunk in February, because the books are already reconciled. The return takes us an hour during our busiest time."

As Padar has outlined in her *Radical CPA* book, successful accounting practices are embracing four "Radical" values that transform firms so that they are no longer too busy doing the accounting work to be a trusted advisor. These values are:

- ✓ Technology/Using the cloud
- ✓ Communication/Becoming a "social" business
- ✓ Pricing/Offering value
- ✓ Process/Altering workflows to provide a better client experience

TECHNOLOGY/USING THE CLOUD

A major requirement of future-ready firms is that they develop a business model that layers on cloud-based technology to allow the firm to scale and be more profitable.

"Think about what you're selling, who you're servicing, and build a new model around that, and then use tools to implement that," she says. "Firms try to insert new tools into the old process, and then they'll say it doesn't work. Of course it doesn't work, because the model is broken. You're not selling what people want; you're selling a compliance document and then putting this tool on top of it, and nobody wants to buy it because you did the wrong thing."

Future-ready firms also groom clients to use cloud technology themselves. "We're a 100 percent cloud firm, so if you're not working with us in the cloud, you're not working with us," Padar says. Allowing a client to continue using a desktop version of QuickBooks really does the client no favors, since the accounting firm can't provide the full value of its service and expertise without real-time and continual access to financial data enabled by cloud technology.

"Traditional firms look at technology as a cost of doing business; they don't look at it as part of the process. What should happen is you should treat technology as being part of the productized service you sell, and then you sell the productized service as a whole."

> "Think about what you're selling, who you're servicing, and **build a new model** around that, and then use tools to implement that."

#NextLevelFirm

COMMUNICATION/BECOMING A "SOCIAL" BUSINESS

Padar has developed a strong brand for her firm using online blogging and social media. "I don't go to chamber of commerce meetings," she says. "Because of all I've written and because of my brand I've developed online, prospects just walk in the door."

Also as a result of her brand development, "People know who I am, and they already know what I stand for, so as soon as they call or walk in, it's not 'Tell me about your rates,' it's 'How are we going to work with you?' and that's what being an online social business does."

The next generation of business owners, especially, want to be able to connect whenever and wherever, so using Twitter, Facebook and email to connect with prospects and clients provides them value.

> " Really, aside from accounting and tax, what we end up selling is **peace of mind**, but that's what most accountants don't know how to sell. "

PRICING/OFFERING VALUE

As explained in the examples above, future-ready firms focus the client on the value you provide rather than a one-time service you perform. "People pay for reports they don't understand and they put them in a drawer… and then CPAs wonder why nobody wants to pay for services," says Padar. "They're not paying for reports, they're paying for value."

In the same way that Starbucks has customers willing to pay $4 and $5 for a coffee drink, accountants can resist commoditization of their services by focusing on the value and experience you offer clients. "Really, aside from accounting and tax, what we end up selling is peace of mind, but that's what most accountants don't know how to sell."

PROCESS/ALTERING WORKFLOWS TO PROVIDE A BETTER CLIENT EXPERIENCE

Future-ready firms examine every step of the process of providing a service to clients, and they streamline or automate as much as possible so the accountants can focus on becoming "that trusted advisor on steroids," Padar says. "If you can call your client because you see something happening in real time, the value is exponentially better than someone who's looking at a report that's weeks old."

Client experiences are also improved by accountants who have the skills to talk with clients, write for them and consult them—soft skills that aren't taught in school and need to be developed on the job.

Padar has been preaching her story of being a "Radical" CPA for about six years and sees many firms moving in the right direction. Still, she's amazed at how many "old school" firms see no need to change. "Who's going to buy their firms? If the next generation isn't going to purchase your firm, where's your retirement plan?"

RESOURCES

- *The Radical CPA: New Rules for the Future-Ready Firm*, by Jody Padar (CPA Trendlines, 2014). http://www.theradicalcpa.com/buy-the-book/
- "Why should CPAs be radical?" by Jody Padar, CPA Trendlines. https://goo.gl/z8NGXf
- Sign up for free updates from Jody on her website, The Radical CPA. https://goo.gl/yH1juv
- "Transform client relationships in your accounting firm," Sageworks whitepaper. http://goo.gl/BxH0Ob

Ramp Up Your Tech Know-How

Are you a taxi driver in a world being disrupted by Uber?

If you still rely on desktop solutions, you may be, according to technology guru Doug Sleeter, one of *CPA Practice Advisor's* Top 25 Thought Leaders and *Accounting Today's* Top 100 Most Influential People in Accounting. Accounting firms with an aversion to technology and innovation could get left in the dust—in much the same way as many taxi drivers who have taken a hit from Uber's surging popularity.

"You can be relatively ignorant of technology solutions today, but you cannot afford to be for long," says Sleeter, founder of The Sleeter Group, the largest group of accounting software consultants in the small business accounting profession. "Agility trumps ability. I don't care how good you are at every tax, finance or auditing question; if that's all you do, the world's going to pass you by, just like Uber passed by the taxi driver."

Sleeter says that being a trusted advisor is all about being proactive and strategic with clients—helping them understand financial data that's as close to real-time as possible in order to plan for a successful future. Research shows that clients hire outside accounting firms for their expertise, but they also desire accountants who are proactive rather than reactive about providing strategic advice. Increasingly, Sleeter says, that proactive, strategic advice is tied to technology clients should be using—especially cloud-based and mobile technology.

For example, more than half of small and medium-sized business owners who currently engage a CPA want technology recommendations from their accountant, and more than three-quarters of the owners who plan to engage a CPA want technology recommendations from their accountant, according to The Sleeter Group's 2014 survey.

But accountants who have focused their professional development efforts on staying abreast of compliance-related professional standards and regulatory changes may not be entirely comfortable recommending technology solutions or helping clients plan and implement tech changes. And even if they are, clients may assume your firm isn't prepared to help. Indeed, only 13 percent of business owners in the Sleeter survey consider their accountant to be ahead of the technology curve.

"The pace at which small businesses are using cloud technology is increasing, and I think it is increasing way faster than the pace at which accountants are embracing it," says Sleeter, who founded the leading independent accounting technology expo and conference, Sleetercon (now called Accountex). Adoption of technology in your own firm doesn't solely affect your practice's operations and efficiency. Sleeter suspects there is a growing distance between what the accountant thinks clients want and what they actually want—a gap that points to opportunity for accountants bucking the trend.

Doug Sleeter

Doug Sleeter is an accounting software guru focused on small business solutions. Founder of Sleeter Group, he remains a consultant to the company after it was acquired by Diversified Communications, and he consults for other technology companies serving small businesses. He has been named among CPA Practice Advisor's Top 25 Thought Leaders, Accounting Today's 100 Most Influential People in Accounting and was chosen as Small Business Trends/Small Biz Technology's 2013 Small Business Influencer Champion. Sleeter is publisher and author of numerous books, including The QuickBooks Consultant's Reference Guide.

 @DougSleeter

> Increasingly, Sleeter says, that proactive, strategic advice is tied to technology clients should be using—especially **cloud-based and mobile technology**.

Accountants who take a deep dive into what their clients want will be able to retain clients and grow revenue for their firms. How do you do this? How can you ramp up your technology know-how in order to meet your clients' needs and become that trusted advisor? Sleeter has this advice:

BE A QUARTERBACK

Accountants should put themselves in the role of quarterback instead of playing every position on the field, and this applies to technological expertise as well, according to Sleeter. "The most trusted advisor doesn't have to have all of the answers," he says. "The most trusted advisor has to become that partner who thinks about the client's business and finds solutions—some of which you provide and others you partner with others for."

Clients generally don't have the best insight into compliance, tax or business processes and technology solutions for efficiently running their businesses. That's where accountants can be proactive. "Most businesses are run by entrepreneurs with that entrepreneurial mindset: that person has a particular mindset or passion or skill and they want to spend all of their time doing that, just like we want to spend all of our time doing accounting or tax or advisory work," Sleeter says. Accountants who understand which technology solutions can help the client will have an advantage. "You become the giant filter that says, 'For you, these are the tools we recommend.'"

LEARN, LEARN, LEARN

Even if your firm decides to act as a filter of technology options rather than as a provider and implementer of solutions, a certain level of expertise is required. "You can't even play the quarterback position if you don't understand what the wide receiver does," Sleeter says.

As soon as your firm hits a period that is less busy, focus on gaining education about various technology options. "Get out and attend conferences and web events, and immerse yourself among peers who are strong in that area," he says. He suggests attending three or four conferences a year and participating in web events hosted by credible vendors or other sources that aren't just selling but are also providing information about a specific challenge your clients or firm faces.

FOCUS ON THE VALUE

In football, part of the quarterback's role is knowing the team so well that you can utilize teammates' talents for the biggest advantage. Accounting firms should be proactive about knowing clients, too, so that they provide the most value. "You study their business; you know their business better than they do in the area you're consulting on," he says.

55% of respondents who currently engage a CPA want technology recommendations from their accountant.

80% of participants who plan to engage a CPA want technology recommendations from their accountant.

The Sleeter Group, "What SMBs Want" Research

#NextLevelFirm

One way to ensure you are offering the technology-related expertise and services that create the most value for clients is to survey clients about business processes and how they currently use technology, Sleeter says. Do they hand write checks? Do they use online banking? How much paper do they use? Numerous online sites, such as Survey Monkey, Survey Planet, Zoho, SurveyGizmo and Google forms offer free or low-cost methods of creating simple surveys quickly.

Taking steps to ramp up your tech know-how is good for your firm's current business and for the value of your firm in the future, Sleeter says. Firms that eventually want to sell to an outsider will have little to offer if they've failed to remain technologically relevant. "If you're getting out in a year and you're old school and haven't done anything with the cloud or technology, you might think your firm is worth perhaps one times revenue," he says. "But if your firm still runs on old technology with tons of paper and people-intensive processes, why wouldn't the buyer just start their own firm as opposed to writing you a check for your firm?"

RESOURCES

- "How the PC nearly destroyed the accounting profession," by Doug Sleeter, Sleeter Report. http://goo.gl/vH2Xib
- "Becoming the most trusted advisor," by Doug Sleeter, Sleeter Report, Part I (http://goo.gl/8Bsspu) and Part II (http://goo.gl/Ce3SC0).
- Sleeter's columns on CPA Practice Advisor. http://goo.gl/6wFxyS
- "Technology overload: Which option is the best for me?" Sageworks blog. https://goo.gl/aKbn9k

#NextLevelFirm

Practical Advice for Scaling a Valuation Practice

Business valuation has been a popular growth avenue pursued by accounting firms in recent years as they look to expand advisory relationships and as millions of retiring baby boomer business owners generate demand.

Ramping up this service efficiently, however, can be challenging. Someone who understands this challenge is Gary R. Trugman, a CPA and accredited valuation professional who has performed valuations for more than 30 years and who wrote the AICPA's book, *Understanding Business Valuation: A Practical Guide to Valuing Small to Medium Sized Businesses*.

While Trugman started by doing divorce-related valuations for mom-and-pop businesses, today his Trugman Valuation Associates firm works with large companies, organizations and government agencies (including FINRA and the IRS) and handles engagements involving big stakes litigation. There was very little in the way of valuation software available to help with the process when Trugman first started offering valuation services. As a result, he developed his own spreadsheet templates—something he estimates has cost him as much as $400,000 in cumulative billable hours.

"A lot of the process really becomes: How can you be efficient in what you're doing but be thorough at the same time?" says Trugman.

His best advice on scaling a valuation practice efficiently is to focus on:

- ✓ Educating your firm
- ✓ Developing a niche
- ✓ Utilizing and implementing technology
- ✓ Leveraging staff and
- ✓ Implementing checks and balances

Gary R. Trugman
CPA/ABV, MCBA, ASA, MVS

Gary R. Trugman is the President of Trugman Valuation Associates Inc., a business valuation and economic damages firm with offices in Plantation, Fla., and Parsippany, N.J. He is Chairman of the American Society of Appraisers' Constitution and Bylaws Committee and a member of its Business Valuation Committee, and he has been on numerous committees of national and state CPA and valuation associations/societies.

He authored the textbook Understanding Business Valuation, coauthored several other textbooks, and has authored numerous educational courses and articles. He is on the faculty of the National Judicial College and has testified throughout the country in both federal and state courts.

EDUCATION

Developing and scaling a valuation practice is difficult to do without having a good education about the industry, says Trugman, who himself continues to read voraciously about changes in the valuation space. He recommends finding many different educational offerings by different organizations. "You need to consider the courses from the American Society of Appraisers, NACVA, IBA, AICPA—as much education as somebody can get," he says. And he suggests reading the staples of business valuation instruction, including his book and *Valuing a Business: The Analysis and Appraisal of*

#NextLevelFirm

Practical Advice for Scaling a Valuation Practice | 43

Closely Held Companies by Shannon Pratt, as well as *Financial Valuation: Applications and Models*, by James R. Hitchner.

"Be well rounded in the sources, and look at as many different things as you can," he says. "Go to as many presentations as you can."

A NICHE

Typically, accountants cannot readily transition from providing a valuation for a local hardware store to providing a valuation for a chain the size of the Home Depot, so it's important to identify a focus for the practice in order to scale it, Trugman says. "The sizes of businesses are very different, so part of what somebody really has to do is understand what their own sweet spot is and recognize that and don't try to do everything," he says. "If you do try to do everything, you're not going to do anything well, and at the end of the day, you're going to commit malpractice."

On a related note, Trugman recommends that firms set up a separate division focused solely on valuation (so long as the board of accountancy in your state allows it). Doing so conveys the singular focus of the practice, thus bolstering credibility and trust among prospects. "I used to have a traditional CPA practice, and when we set up Trugman Valuation Associates, one reason we did is that doing valuation as a small accounting firm had a bad connotation, but if you were a small boutique, now you became an expert. From a marketing standpoint, it's unbelievable the difference it made."

TECHNOLOGY

Trugman believes technology can play an important role in scaling a business. Standardizing processes and protecting against human error boosts efficiency and accuracy.

While he uses templates developed by his firm internally over several decades, Trugman says he'd utilize software if his templates got wiped out or he had to start his business over. "For probably 80 percent of the assignments, I could probably get away most of the time with a commercial package," he says.

It's imperative, however, that software users understand valuation. "People go out and buy a software package and they let the software drive the valuation instead of the other way around, and that's how they get into trouble, because they don't know maybe that software isn't appropriate for a particular kind of job," Trugman says. "Maybe one of the methodologies that the software does happens to be the wrong methodology for that particular assignment."

Users must ensure that the valuation technology is appropriate for the size of businesses that will be valued. "You don't want to buy a package that is basically geared to do smaller jobs if you're valuing Fortune 500 companies,"

he says. "Your methodologies are different, the levels of sophistication are different. You've got to be careful with that."

Software should also be flexible enough to allow the valuation professional to make warranted changes in a specific engagement. "There are so many ways you can calculate discount rates. If the software does a traditional build-up method but the build-up method's not appropriate, you'd better be able to use something else."

"I'm a big fan of software, because you can't re-set up these templates from scratch every time you do a job," he says. "It's not efficient; the client will never pay you to spend that much time."

LEVERAGING STAFF

In the early days of his practice, Trugman would spread the financials for each engagement and perform the economic and industry research. He did all of the financial analysis and wrote the reports. As the practice has grown, he and partner Linda Trugman (who is also his wife and international president of the American Society of Appraisers) have added staff to handle many of those duties.

Training and educating staff about valuation so that they can take on larger aspects of the engagement provides Trugman time to bring in more business and to manage relationships with law firms or accounting firms that refer cases to the practice. "It gives me a lot of time to deal with the attorneys, strategizing the litigation and doing more high-level work, which I'm able to get a much better hourly rate for," he says. It also provides unique insight that strengthens results.

Scaling a valuation practice requires building up processes to ensure accuracy and thoroughness, Trugman says.

CHECKS AND BALANCES

Scaling a valuation practice requires building up processes to ensure accuracy and thoroughness, Trugman says. He and his team have created a manual for performing a valuation so that there is a consistent reference point for everyone involved in the engagement. He also uses other "checks and balances" to force standardization and ensure that his team's work is accurate. For example, in addition to proofing each valuation report for accuracy and cosmetics, the firm checks by calculator the accuracy of every section that includes numbers and calculations. Trugman and his staff have also developed workflow and report checklists. "We ask things like, 'Did you normalize cash? Did you look at inventory?'" Trugman says. "By adapting these things into checklists, I'm forcing staff to think about these things as they're going through the process."

#NextLevelFirm

Practical Advice for Scaling a Valuation Practice | 45

RESOURCES

- Publications authored by Trugman or his partner can be found on the firm's website. http://trugmanvaluation.com/valuation/publications/
- "Valuing the very small company," by Gary R. Trugman, Trugman Valuation website. http://goo.gl/igIE0x
- "Business valuation fundamentals," by Gary R. Trugman, Trugman Valuation website. http://goo.gl/xZpSvr
- "Common errors found in valuation reports," Sageworks practice aid. http://goo.gl/a3lgCf

From Good to Great: Overcome 3 Obstacles to Accounting Firm Growth

For a lot of accounting firms, life is pretty good. The firms provide high quality, necessary services. Clients are generally happy, and those services produce reliable work, healthy income and a comfortable lifestyle for firm partners and associates. Many firms, however, could have it even better, according to Joe Woodard, who provides training, networking and technology consulting to accountants and other small business advisors.

Woodard says that firms could be much more profitable and achieve more satisfaction by setting transformative-level goals with their corporate clients. Instead of simply providing tax returns (compliance services) or financial statements (backward-looking services) that are important but not proactive, transformative services provide a measureable effect and an increase in the client's wealth.

Building a transformative practice—what Woodard calls "The Epic Practice"—requires a paradigm shift for many accounting professionals, a radical change in focus for the whole of the firm.

"Getting people to go from bad to good is easy," Woodard says. "Motivating people to go from good to great is extremely difficult, because sometimes in their mind, good is good enough."

Woodard says that the current accounting technology landscape has made it easier to traverse the otherwise Herculean breach between good and great. The way he sees it, technology and the practices of accountants in recent years have evolved to a point where they are capable of producing the "Holy Grail" for small businesses. Woodard's "Holy Grail" is financial information that is both accurate and real-time. To be actionable, financial data must be both current and accurate. This combination has eluded the profession for decades, perhaps centuries.

While accountants have always produced accurate data, under traditional write up models, that data has been typically available long after the quarter or year has ended and is, therefore, of limited use. If the small business takes responsibility for their own bookkeeping, the records are often current but are sorely incomplete and inaccurate.

Joe Woodard

Joe Woodard is CEO of Woodard Companies, which include: Woodard Events, Woodard Consulting, Woodard Network, Woodard Groups and Woodard Institute. As an author, consultant, business coach and national speaker, he has trained over 75,000 accounting and business professionals in areas of practice development, changing technology trends, strategic consulting and how to maximize the use of accounting software in their practices. He has been named to Accounting Today's 100 Most Influential People in Accounting and CPA Practice Advisor's 40 Under 40 awards.

  @joewoodard

> " Getting people to go from bad to good is easy, **motivating people to go from good to great is extremely difficult.** "

#NextLevelFirm

"This is the first time in human history that we've been able to consistently gain access to the financial information we need to confidently provide forward-looking, proactive metrics," Woodard says. "It is the best time for an accountant to be alive."

Woodard believes that embracing technology can help accounting firms overcome three important barriers to growth—three obstacles to "greatness."

The first obstacle is a ceiling on the amount of revenue a firm can generate. "You can only keypunch so fast," he notes, adding that the only way to break through that ceiling is to significantly reduce costs through automation technologies while at the same time providing new, highly valued services for clients. This combination will significantly increase profits. "What would you do with another $200,000 a year in your bottom line? Would you pay off your house? Would you pay off your children's college fund? Would you put it all into a 401k? Would you take a trip to Europe?"

A second barrier to growth is the fact that "bread and butter" accounting services tied to payroll, sales tax and other functions can already be automated or even outsourced by technology and by providers tangent to the profession that are specialized and highly scalable, yet many practices still offer these services in essentially the same form as 10 years ago. This means continued pricing pressure and high client turnover.

Finally, less proactive services like bookkeeping, assurance and tax preparation prevent firms from focusing on the "transformative consulting" that their clients desperately need, according to Woodard. When both the accountant and the client are focused on the past (e.g., bookkeeping and compliance), you don't have time and the client doesn't have the budget to focus on business growth and development, he notes.

How does technology address these barriers? By providing improved collaboration, innovation and automation.

Cloud (or Internet-based) solutions like Google Hangouts and interactive chat make it possible to provide clients with quick answers or to discuss a project with colleagues without having to pick up the phone. Other solutions like Dropbox, Box and SmartVault make it easy to securely share documents so work can move forward quickly. Project-management solutions that intelligently route email, catalog client correspondence and create tasks are significantly streamlining workflow for accounting firms and making the relationships with clients high touch. "Technologies that were affordable only to the largest CPA firms in the world only 10 years ago are now within the reach of sole practitioners. This level of empowerment for small and emerging firms is extremely encouraging for the profession and for the small businesses it serves," Woodard says.

Using these collaborative solutions, accountants can have access to documents they need for working on client accounts anytime, anywhere; they can also easily access resources that improve efficiency and responsiveness.

> Woodard believes that **embracing technology** can help accounting firms overcome three important barriers to growth, so that the firm can **transform from the 'status quo' of good to next-level great.**

#NextLevelFirm

Cloud-based technology also fuels innovation. Cloud solutions have a product development cycle as short as four to six weeks, while desktop solutions typically provide significant enhancements only once a year. As a result, accounting firms consistently have access to new innovations and can provide incremental improvements to the firm's processes throughout the year, Woodard notes.

Finally, technology solutions are automating bookkeeping processes. This is happening most notably with intelligent banking imports, expense reporting, payroll and accounts payable management. And, automation is an ever-expanding category which, Woodard predicts, will replace on a consistent basis over 80 percent of the bookkeeping process in the near future. This level of automation frees the firm's capacity to focus on the higher-value services that their clients want—or at the very least need. These solutions can even handle benchmarking, business analytics and management consulting so that the firm can drive up the value of its services even as costs come down due to automation.

"All of that is only made possible if the profession embraces these cutting-edge technologies and fully leverages them to the benefit of its business clients. We have the tools and we have a mandate to transform small business. Accountants who combine the two will become 'The Epic Practice.'"

RESOURCES

- "What is an Epic Practice?" by Joe Woodard, Insightful Accountant website. http://goo.gl/UlRGcs
- Video: Move Beyond the Technology, Accounting Today's website. http://goo.gl/6BXMfo
- "Grow my accounting practice, episode 1," podcast with Joe Woodard, Profit First Professionals website. http://goo.gl/5V4UVW
- "A QuickBooks ProAdvisor reality TV show", by Joe Woodard, Insightful Accountant website. http://goo.gl/LhvwDu
- "1 Easy way to go from tax accountant to trusted advisor," Sageworks blog. https://goo.gl/T0cZZZ

Mapping Your Tech Strategy

The process of incorporating technology into your practice and using it to expand advisory services can seem daunting. However, technology industry veteran Erik Asgeirsson has valuable advice to help firms tackle this initiative.

Asgeirsson, president and CEO of CPA.com, the technology subsidiary of the AICPA, says that before trying to answer the questions of **how** and **when** your firm will select and incorporate technology, make sure you've answered two questions that are even more important:

- What is the firm's strategy for becoming trusted business advisors?
- Who will lead these efforts with a dedicated focus?

"We've seen some firms [have to] come back to those initial questions if they start just with the technology," says Asgeirsson, who is regularly listed on *Accounting Today's* annual list of the Top 100 Most Influential People in Accounting. He explains that many firms with a piecemeal strategy will move quickly to evaluate and sign up with technology vendors. "What we've found," Asgeirsson says, "is that [firms who do this] will probably have some real adoption or onboarding issues in building out that practice area."

"It's very difficult to make the 'how' operating decisions before you've decided on the 'what,'" he says. "It seems very basic, but it's something we've seen a lot of firms fall into the trap of—jumping first to the discussion of the technology versus the business strategy."

WHAT IS THE FIRM'S STRATEGY?

Because of the array of service opportunities available as a result of technology, Asgeirsson recommends identifying and understanding the firm's strategy as it relates to advisory services as a first step.

Cloud-based technology has brought the small-business practice areas of accounting firms into the Information Age. It allows accounting firms to provide the client with ongoing, real-time financial data on the business results, along with CFO-like advice or other advisory services, Asgeirsson says. Twenty years ago, the trusted advisor's data and insight were more asynchronous, so the advice might take place weeks or months after the financial period ended. Now, however, firms can combine cloud accounting, bill-payment and payroll solutions with financial intelligence solutions—Sageworks' ProfitCents is one example—to create business process outsourcing and other virtual CFO-type services, he says.

Erik Asgeirsson
MBA

Erik Asgeirsson, CEO and president at CPA.com, has more than 20 years of experience in leading technology organizations and driving business growth. Over the past 10 years he has driven CPA.com's focus on cloud computing and the transforming opportunities available to accounting firms and their business clients. During his tenure, CPA.com has added several new lines of business and is a leading change agent for driving technology adoption in the accounting profession.

He is regularly listed in Accounting Today's annual Top 100 Most Influential People in Accounting, and is a member of the DigitalNow Advisory Group, which counsels business leaders on opportunities in the digital age.

  @ErikAsgeirsson

> " It's very difficult to make the **'how'** operating decisions before you've decided on the **'what.'** "

#NextLevelFirm

"Twenty years ago CPAs were just working in a very off-line kind of business advisor capacity, not really giving [clients] the immediate intelligence that a cloud accounting solution with dashboards gives to their clients."

Determining the strategy first ensures that the technology actually supports the firm's needs.

When the firm is considering a strategy related to advisory services, Asgeirsson says, "You're thinking about things such as your vertical focus, the niche you're going to play in. Really understanding where your strengths are but at the same time also looking at the opportunity of those different verticals, making sure that your strengths and opportunities are well aligned."

Some firms have identified strategies related to serving multiple needs of an industry, such as the restaurant industry or private schools. Others have developed strategies aimed at certain markets, such as venture capital or private equity firms that may need outsourced CFO services for companies they purchase.

WHO WILL LEAD THESE EFFORTS?

The next important step in tackling technology is identifying the players who will be able to provide the dedicated focus on the firm's strategy, according to Asgeirsson.

"Do you have the right person to be the leader of this advisory area? Do you have someone you can staff internally, or do you need to go bring somebody new in that area?"

Firms that have found successes in trusted advisor services have "found the right individual to go build that and they've given that individual some dedicated focus related to it," Asgeirsson says. But firms cannot simply morph a division that is providing standard accounting services into their "advisory practice," he says. By doing this, firms run the risk of attempting to fit a square peg into a round hole. "Retooling a non-strategic part of the business doesn't necessarily deliver success," he says.

> " Twenty years ago CPAs were just working in a very off-line kind of business advisor capacity, not really giving [clients] the immediate intelligence that a cloud accounting solution with dashboards gives to their clients. "

NOW WHAT?

Asgeirsson acknowledges that these two steps can take some time. CPA.com has a wide range of resources to help in these areas, and once a firm has settled on its strategy and talent, CPA.com also has resources for evaluating and buying technology solutions. For example, CPA.com partnered with business technology review site TrustRadius to develop a buyer's guide for business process outsourcing software. It also developed a whitepaper with business technology strategist Geoffrey Moore to outline actions that firms can take to transform their practices using digital technologies. CPA.com also has links to numerous workshops and webinars that tie technology to trusted advisor services.

Asgeirsson says his experience with firms has shown that technology can be "really quite powerful," particularly for firms trying to move into advisory services. But technology shouldn't be viewed as a substitute for strategy.

"There's a whole new world of providing these services," he says. "Technology is an integral part of a firm's strategy."

> "There's a whole new world of providing these services.
>
> **Technology is an integral part of a firm's strategy.**"

RESOURCES

- Trust Radius Accounting Firm BPO Software Guide. https://goo.gl/ggJCWm
- *Harnessing the Power of the Cloud* by Geoffrey Moore. http://goo.gl/Ozb9ob
- CPA.com educational resources. http://www.cpa.com/education
- "Advantages of software as a service," Sageworks infographic. http://goo.gl/Fp14TE

Mapping Your Tech Strategy

#NextLevelFirm

Learn how your firm can differentiate, streamline processes and build a stronger advisory practice with ProfitCents and Sageworks Valuation Solution.

One-Minute Product Overview Videos

web.sageworks.com/next-level-accountant/video-walkthrough/

Close the communication gap with your clients by providing a comprehensive business analysis with easy-to-understand narrative, graphs, ratios and industry comparisons. Financial professionals use ProfitCents automated reports to attract prospects and strengthen client relationships by providing data-rich benchmarking, strategic planning and streamlined audit engagements. ProfitCents is built on the largest real-time database of private-company financials in the United States, which includes data on more than 1,400 industries and industry specific KPIs for analyzing operational efficiency.

sageworks | Valuation Solution

Streamline valuation workflow while generating accurate, professional reports using the income, market and asset approaches, modeled after SSVS No. 1 standards. Scale existing firm processes to increase realization rates and create opportunities for growth.

Find more articles, whitepapers and practice aids for developing a "Next-Level" firm.

Visit Sageworks.com for Accounting and Business Valuation resources:

- **Accounting resources** | www.sageworks.com/cpa/whitepapers.aspx
- **Business Valuation resources** | www.sageworks.com/valuation/resources.aspx

---

#NextLevelFirm

866.603.7029 EXT **2**

sales@sageworks.com

www.ingramcontent.com/pod-product-compliance
Lightning Source LLC
Chambersburg PA
CBHW050805180526
45159CB00004B/1560